steps

A basic English course

3

Paul Groves
John Griffin
Nigel Grimshaw

Longman

LONGMAN GROUP UK LIMITED
Longman House
Burnt Mill, Harlow, Essex CM20 2JE, England and
Associated companies throughout the World.

First published 1983
Third impression 1986
ISBN 0 582 20147 0

Set in 11/12 pt Linotron 202 Souvenir Light

*Produced by Longman Singapore Publishers Pte Ltd
Printed in Singapore*

Steps
a basic English course
Book 1 0 582 20145 4
     2 0 582 20146 2
     3 0 582 20147 0
     4 0 582 20148 9

Steps skills books
The alphabet at work   0 582 21995 7
Be a writer   0 582 21997 3
Write in sentences   0 582 21996 5

Contents

✓ = *mark these yourself.*

1 The robot – conjunctions

Factory's robot kills a worker

A robot has killed a worker. Details of the accident were revealed yesterday. Kenji Urada, aged 37, entered a prohibited area around the robot to repair it.

A wire-mesh fence around the robot shut off its power supply if anyone opened it. Instead of unhooking it though, Urada jumped over the fence. He set the robot on manual control. Accidentally, he then brushed against the on-switch. The claw of the robot pushed him against a cutting machine. Other workers were unable to stop the robot's action.

The company said that the robot has now been removed from the assembly line. A man-high fence has been erected around two other robots.

News of the accident will cause concern to employees in Japanese industry because 20,000 robots a year are being put in factories. Trade unions in Japan have given the robots a mixed reception. On the one hand, they are relieved that robots are taking over some of the monotonous and dirty jobs on the assembly line. On the other hand, they are afraid that robots will take away people's jobs.

Robot-building firms are working on a new kind of 'smart' robot. This will be capable of many different jobs on the assembly line.

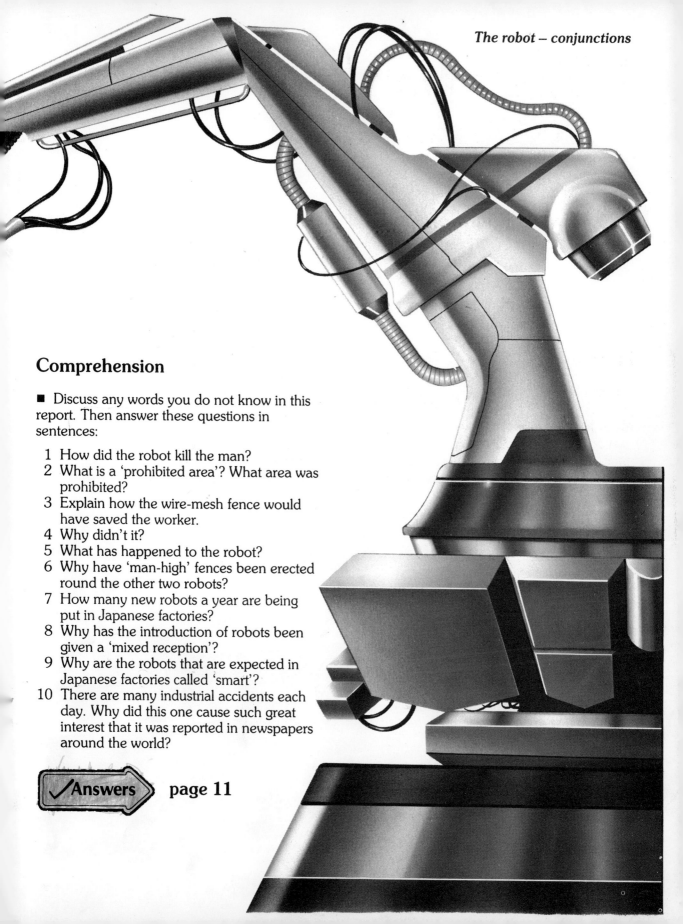

Comprehension

■ Discuss any words you do not know in this report. Then answer these questions in sentences:

1 How did the robot kill the man?
2 What is a 'prohibited area'? What area was prohibited?
3 Explain how the wire-mesh fence would have saved the worker.
4 Why didn't it?
5 What has happened to the robot?
6 Why have 'man-high' fences been erected round the other two robots?
7 How many new robots a year are being put in Japanese factories?
8 Why has the introduction of robots been given a 'mixed reception'?
9 Why are the robots that are expected in Japanese factories called 'smart'?
10 There are many industrial accidents each day. Why did this one cause such great interest that it was reported in newspapers around the world?

✓ **Answers** page 11

Questions on the pictures

■ Now look at the two pictures and the one on the left.

a Actual robots don't look like this (page 8). Why are they made to look like this in stories and films?

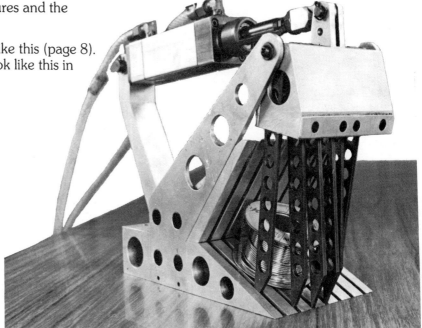

b These are actual robots (page 9).
What part of the body does each of them represent?
What do you think their job is?

Discussion

A robot is only a machine. Why have people regarded robots with suspicion? What jobs might robots do in the future? Would you like a robot in your house? What jobs would you like it to do?

Write a letter

■ Write a letter to a robot maker. Ask him or her to design a robot to do various things in your house or flat. Think of the jobs you or your family do not like to do. You might like your shoes cleaned for example.
Make the letter quite serious.

■ Write a letter to a robot maker. Ask him or her to design a robot to do silly things in your house or flat. Do you have trouble getting out of bed in the morning for example?
Make the letter funny.

Punctuation – sentences

Always write your stories in sentences.

■ Punctuate this piece by Alnaz. Remember that each group of words that make sense is a sentence. Put in all the capital letters and full-stops:

> when my house was finished i built my last robot it was a robot to lift me gently out of bed in the morning quickly it took all my clothes out of the wardrobe and dressed me then it made me a cup of tea downstairs Robot No. 1 was cooking my breakfast in the lounge Robot No. 2 was doing the cleaning while in the garage Robot No. 3 was reversing my car out

 **✓Answers** page 17

Writing about robots

■ Using sentences, write a piece called either:
'Chased by a robot'
or 'Robot in the home'

■ John chose the 'Chased by a robot' title. Here is part of his piece of writing:

> I saw this shiny thing deep in the wood and I did not like it and I could hear a humming sound coming from it and I could see two enormous red eyes and then it began to move and I was surprised to see that it was more than three metres tall and . . . .

Can you see the mistake John has made? He has joined all his sentences together with the word **and**.

✓Answers *Questions on page 7*

1 The claw of the robot pushed him against a cutting machine. **1**
2 It is a place where you are not supposed to go. **1**
   The area round the robot was prohibited. **1**
3 A wire-mesh fence around the robot would have shut off the robot's power supply when unhooked. **2**
4 Urada did not unhook it. He jumped over it. **2**
5 It has been removed from the assembly line. **2**
6 They have been erected so workers cannot jump over them. **2**
7 20,000 robots a year are being put in Japanese factories. **2**
8 They like the idea that it will stop workers having to do monotonous and dirty jobs. **1**
   They do not like the idea that it will take away people's jobs. **1**
9 They are called smart because they will do many jobs. **2**
10 This caused interest because it was about the first worker to be killed by a robot. **1**

Total marks = **18**

Using *and*

If we take all the **ands** out of John's story it will read like this:

> I could see this shiny thing deep in the wood. I did not like it. I could hear a humming sound coming from it. I could see two enormous red eyes. Then it began to move. I was surprised to see that it was more than three metres tall.

This is an improvement but it sounds jerky. This can be boring in a long story. What you can do is to join *some* of your sentences together with **and**.

Discussion

And is called a conjunction. Which sentences in John's piece do you think sound right if joined together by **and**?

Joining sentences

And

■ Join the following sentences together by **and** only if you think that they go together. Copy out the other ones as two separate sentences if you think that they would sound silly joined by **and**:

1 | He had hit his thumb with a hammer. | It hurt very much.

2 | She had been on her bike all day. | She was very tired.

3 | I am fourteen tomorrow. | My brother likes chocolates.

4 | There was an electrical fault in the kitchen. | It set the house on fire.

5 | The skier came down the hill very fast. | She had had kippers for breakfast.

 **Answers** page 13

But

Another sentence joining word is **but**. You could say:

I fell out of bed **and** it did not hurt me.
But it would be better to say:
I fell out of bed **but** it did not hurt me.

In the second sentence **but** is used because something unexpected happens.

■ Replace **and** with **but** in these sentences if you think **but** sounds better. Copy out the remainder leaving the **and** in:

1 He asked me to go out with him and I could not go.
2 They are bottom of the league at the moment and they will soon reach the top.
3 I did not understand the homework and I managed to complete some of it.
4 My mother put a new shade on the lamp and it made the room look better.
5 I worked hard for five years and I thought I had earned my money.

 **Answers** **page 13**

So

Another common joining word in sentences is **so**:

I got up early **so** I could be in front of the queue. This joining word suggests a reason for doing something.

■ Complete these sentences by adding a sensible ending.
Do not begin with 'that':

1 He helped his mother so . . . .
2 There was no water for ten miles so . . . .
3 She went to the post office so . . . .
4 The runner kept getting the stitch so . . . .
5 She wanted to get there before her sister so . . . .

■ Look back at the robot story you wrote. See if you have used **and, but** or **so** to join up any sentences.

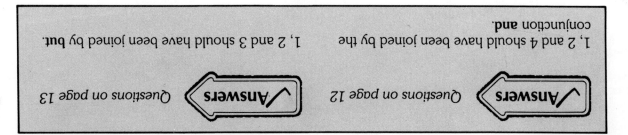

 Answers *Questions on page 12*

1, 2 and 4 should have been joined by the conjunction **and.**

Answers *Questions on page 13*

1, 2 and 3 should have been joined by **but.**

More joining words

Here are some more joining words. They help your writing to become more varied and exact:

**because   if   when   where   until
though   before   unless   as**

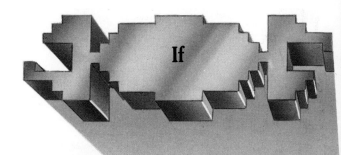

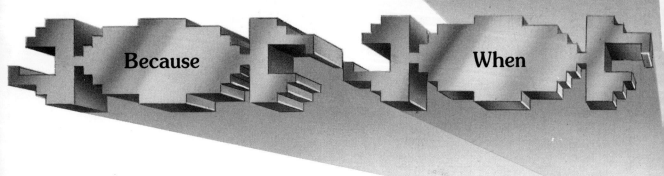

Because

There was no need to tell lies **because** his mother knew the truth.

- Complete these sentences:

1 I do not like to stay out late because . . . .
2 The team lost the match because . . . .
3 She went to hospital because . . . .
4 There is no need to tell your father because . . . .
5 I hate you because . . . .

If

I do not like to go out in these shoes **if** it is raining.

1 He said he would not help his sister if . . . .
2 The manager would only pick him if . . . .
3 Please bring the washing in if . . . .
4 Do not touch it if . . . .
5 She always stayed in bed if . . . .

When

I like to wear a hat **when** it is very hot.

1 You must come home when . . . .
2 He fell to the floor when . . . .
3 She received a great cheer when . . . .
4 The postman was very surprised when . . . .
5 The car came off the road when . . . .

Where

There is a tree **where** the road bends.

1 Can you show me where the . . . .
2 Put the bandage where . . . .
3 She did not know where she . . . .
4 I know an ideal place to picnic where . . . .
5 They all know the house where . . . .

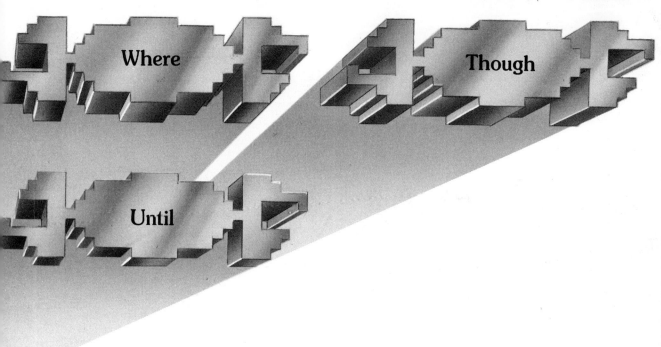

Until

You must not go out **until** your father gets home.

1 I held on until I . . . .
2 They could not score until the . . . .
3 They pushed and pushed the car until it . . . .
4 She felt she could not see her friend until she . . . .
5 The climber held onto the rope until he . . . .

Though

I recognized him at the station **though** I only had a photo of him.

1 They still went out for the day though . . . .
2 You must not tell me the truth though . . . .
3 You must still do it though . . . .
4 He still felt ill though . . . .
5 There were not enough helpers though . . . .

'although' has a similar meaning and can be used as an alternative to 'though'.

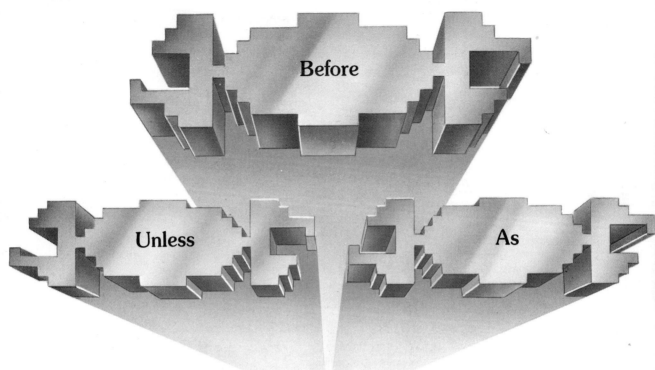

Before

You must clean up **before** your mother gets home.

1 She read five chapters of the book before she . . . .
2 The starter checked his pistol before he . . . .
3 The farmer ploughed the field before it . . . .
4 She had to obtain a passport before she . . . .
5 I want to know the truth before I . . . .

Unless

I do not like to work hard **unless** I have had a good breakfast.

1 I will keep you in unless . . . .
2 We will not be able to complete the match unless . . . .
3 The space ship would crash unless . . . .
4 You cannot go out tonight unless . . . .
5 The explorer knew she would die unless . . . .

As

He could not go out **as** he had not done his homework

1 You must stay in as . . . .
2 She ran out of the room as . . . .
3 You must help your brother as . . . .
4 She had to send her a birthday present as . . . .
5 He went to see his grandma as . . . .

■ Look back through your robot story and check whether you have used any of these joining words.

Another way is to begin with a conjunction or joining word:

Because his mother knew the truth there was no need to tell lies.
If it is raining, I do not like to go out in these shoes.

■ Check through the sentences you have just written in this section. Write out again any that sound sensible with the conjunction put first. *Do not write out any that sound silly.*

Picking the best joining word

■ Use the best conjunction to join these sentences:

1 Do not take off the top.
  You have shaken the bottle.
2 Do not go out tonight.
  You have permission from your mother or father.
3 They ran for shelter.
  The rain came down.
4 Try and finish the work.
  The teacher comes in.
5 She still went to school.
  She had toothache.
6 Do not dive in.
  The last swimmer touches the end of the bath.
7 You cannot have any more.
  The saucepan is empty.
8 There were great floods.
  It rained for ten days.
9 I do not know the place.
  The murder took place.

Adding sentences

■ Add a sentence to each of the following. Pick the best joining word for each one. Do not use 'and'.
Make sure that your final sentence makes sense.

1 Let him alone. . . .
2 We will go to the sea. . . .
3 Keep her head raised . . .
4 Do not start the race . . .
5 You cannot keep pigeons. . . .
6 She still bought her a present . . .
7 Do not set it alight . . .
8 You will find the best fish . . .
9 He felt he was dying . . .
10 It is not wise to go swimming . . .
11 He went to the cafe . . .
12 Do not overtake . . .
13 Will you write to me . . .?
14 The fog was very thick . . .
15 This may hurt . . .

Now write ten sentences of your own using some of the conjunctions you have found in this chapter.

Answering *Why* questions

The answer to the question:

Why did the robot kill the man?
is not:
Because he accidentally touched the switch.
This is not a sentence.

The answer should be:
The robot killed the man **because** he touched the switch.

Always use the question to help you make a complete sentence answer.

■ Answer these questions in a sentence using **because**:

1 Why is the newspaper report not a pleasant one?
2 Why was the area prohibited?
3 Why are the Japanese putting robots in their factories?
4 Why do they want new robots?
5 Why would your family like a robot to do the housework?

 **Answers** *Questions on page 11*

You should have put full-stops after these words: last robot; morning; dressed me; cup of tea; breakfast; cleaning; my car out.
There should be a capital for the first word of the passage **when** and after each full stop.

The Horse

Chapter 1

1 Jane first saw the horse in a paddock near the slow-moving river in the meadow. The paddock had coloured poles in it and drums for the horse to jump over. A girl in full riding kit and a very straight back was taking it over the jumps. Jane hung over the fence and watched. If

5 only she could have a horse like that.

But this horse looked too good to be owned by anybody. It was fifteen hands high and its coat was of a fine chestnut silky sheen; it was all curves and flowing muscles with the legs delicate and dainty. She felt sure it could win the Grand National. She was thinking of herself

10 riding to victory on it when the girl rode up and tapped the fence with her crop. 'Hey you! Must you stand there gawping like that? It's putting off Tiger. Don't you know this is private land?'

Her stomach tingled deep with resentment. She wanted to say: 'Who do you think you are, you stuck-up madam?' Instead she said:

15 'Sorry,' and moved quickly away.

At tea she said: 'I saw a lovely horse today, Mum. Do you think I could have a horse one day?'

'I'm worrying about where your next pair of shoes is coming from,' said her mother. 'Don't talk so daft.'

Comprehension

■ Write the answers to these questions on the story. The storyline numbers on the right will help you:

1 What conjunctions can you spot in Chapter 1? Which can you see that join sentences? Make a list. Do the same when you read through the next three chapters.
2 What is a paddock? Use a dictionary if you like. (2)
3 How can we tell that the girl who owns the horse is proud and unpleasant? (11–12)
4 What characteristics would you find in a stuck-up person?
5 Was Jane right to ask her mother for a horse? (16–17)

Chapter 2

20   The horse came into her dreams, only it was white with a long flowing mane. It came flying in on a cloud in a moon-steeped sky.

One day the thought came to her. If she could not have a horse at least she could pet Tiger and give him some titbits. She would go in the early morning before the girl was up.

25   She woke up at five the next morning and crept down the stairs. There was half a stale loaf in the larder and she had some Polos as well. She gently closed the front door.

She ran through the dingy streets to the dew-soaked field of the meadow. Her shoes were all soggy and stained with buttercup yellow

30   but she felt as light as she did in her dream. An early morning fisherman smiled at her as she tore by. Finally she reached the paddock.

The girl was there brushing Tiger. 'Hey you there. Isn't there any time of the day I can ride my horse without you gawping? I'll have the

35   police on you.'

She rushed headlong through the meadow. 'What's up, duck?' said the fisherman. But she was past him and at her own door before she stopped running. Her mother was up looking for her and she was very cross. Where had she been? Didn't she know anything could happen

40   to a young girl at that time of day? Just look at her shoes. Where was the bread she was going to make the breakfast toast with?

She told her mother about the horse. Her mother told her not to be so silly and to get back up to bed and stay there for the morning.

Comprehension

6 What two sentences describe how the horse first appears to Jane in a dream? (20–21)

7 What does 'gawping' mean? Is it a fair word to use about Jane? (34)

Chapter

But the horse came strong in her dreams. Her mother's telling-off
45 had no effect on its magnet pull over her. An idea came to her: she
would go at night. The girl would not be there then and she would
have the horse to herself.

She crept out of her bedroom at midnight, clutching her Polos and
some biscuits saved from tea.
50 A full moon shone like the moon of her dreams. She could find her
way across the meadow easily. She felt no fear, only the excitement of
seeing the horse.

She reached the paddock fence. There was the misty outline of
Tiger cropping the moon-turf. 'Tiger! Tiger!' she half whispered, half
55 called.

It came straight away and she fed it with the biscuits. She thrilled to
the touch of its wet mouth and hot breath caressing her fingers. She
stayed for half an hour and then returned home.

She did the same for the next three nights. But on the third the idea
60 came to her that she could ride the horse round the paddock. It stood
close to the fence. She only had to climb up and fling her leg over its
back.

'Tiger,' she said softly. It nuzzled up. She must take this chance. She
swung her leg over. She was riding a horse!
65 Tiger moved slowly at first at a walking pace. She sat up like the girl.
She imagined herself in riding gear. But then Tiger started to trot and
she had to fling her arms round its neck to stay on without a saddle
and bridle. She still had no feeling of fear, only excitement. But then it
leapt the paddock fence!

Comprehension

8 Find out what 'obsessed' means in a
dictionary. Write down one sentence from
the story which suggests that Jane is
obsessed by the horse. (44–46)
9 What does 'nuzzled' mean? Use a
dictionary if you like. (63)
10 Was she brave to try to ride the horse at
night or silly? Say why. (59–60)

Chapter 4

70   She was amazed to find herself still on its back as Tiger galloped across the meadow. She clung round its neck with all her might and dug her knees into its flanks. This was not like the horse of her dreams. Its back was like a board. She felt like a bag of bones. Its breath came in snorts. Rich, musty smells of sweat came to her
75   nostrils. But it was marvellous. It was only when they entered the dark wood that the fear came.

    Now she could not see where they were going. The speed of the horse had not lessened; twigs brushed against her face; she jolted up and down on its back even more. Fear now bit deeply into her.

80   The horse suddenly skidded. This was it. She slid right over its head in a somersault. She seemed to wait for the ground to smash into her back; instead there was a splash as she landed in water. The horse had stopped by the river.

    Even so all the breath was knocked out of her and she felt she must
85   drown as she gulped for air. But the river was not deep and her feet touched the bottom. She dragged her dripping body to the bank. Tiger had galloped away into the night.

    After half an hour of stumbling through the wood she found herself back at the paddock. Tiger was there cropping the grass as if nothing
90   had happened. She ran home.

    Lights were on at her house. Her father was at the door. 'Where have you been?' he shouted and hit her across the face. He was about to do it again as she said nothing but her mother rescued her. In the small sitting room the whole story came out in sobs.

95   Later on she lay in bed. Her mouth bled and she felt bruised all over. But she did not dream that night. She did not dream of the white horse again.

Comprehension

The answers
to all four chapters
are on page 23.

11 In what way was the horse different from the horse of her dreams? (73)

12 When does she start to be really afraid? (75–76)

13 What saves her from being injured? (82)

14 Was her father's punishment fair? Or would you say that she had already been punished? (92)

15 Make up another title for the story instead of 'The Horse'.

Revision and further work

■ Punctuate this passage correctly into sentences and put in any other capital letters:

sonya did not want to get her dress at marks and spencer's because other people at the party might come in the same one she went down the high street so she could look in pearl's window a rolls royce came round the corner where the traffic lights were it mounted the pavement and ran into manfield's window there was a loud crack when it hit the glass if she had been two metres further down the pavement she could have been killed

Now underline the conjunctions.

■ Write your own story about a horse. It could be about a race. It could be about a man who ill-treats a horse and you save it. Describe the horse clearly. Remember to write in sentences.

■ Find ten verbs in 'The Horse' story.

■ Make up five questions for your own robot or horse story. Write them out and give them to a friend who has read your story to answer. Remember the question marks.

■ Put these words into alphabetical order:

conjunction   contradict   conceited

conductor   concert   construction

concussion   conservation   conversation

congratulate.

✓ **Answers**   *Questions on pages 19, 20, 21 and 22*

1 and, if, when, where, as, before, but
Each of these joins sentences. Some are used several times.   **7**
2 A paddock is a small field.   **1**
3 We can tell by the way she talks to Jane. If you have put down any of the things she says score the same mark.   **1**
4 Score for any of these:
They might not speak to you.
They would think they are better than you.   **1**
5 No, she was not right. Her mother was too poor.   **2**
6 The horse came into her dreams, only it was white with a long flowing mane. It came flying in on a cloud in a moon-steeped sky.   **2**
7 It means to look or stare with an open mouth. It is not a fair word. She liked the horse so much.   **2**
8 It means your mind is filled with an

idea and you can think of nothing else.   **1**
The horse came into her dreams, only it was white with a long flowing mane. or
But the horse came strong in her dreams.   **1**
9 Nuzzled means to rub with the nose.   **1**
10 She was silly. She could easily have been killed.   **2**
11 It was a very hard ride. (Its back was like a board).   **2**
12 She starts to be really afraid when she enters the wood.   **1**
13 The water breaks her fall.   **2**
14 It was not fair as she had had a shock. We think she had learned her lesson already. In a way though we admire what she did.   **2**
15 We hope you thought of a good one.
Total marks = **28**

2 Talking to people

Marbury is a town and Dunton End used to be a small village about a mile and a half outside Marbury. The town grew and houses were built at Dunton End. Now Dunton End is a big housing estate and is part of Marbury. The picture shows you what Dunton End looks like now.

Here is a news item from the town paper. *The Marbury Post*

Dunton End development

There are plans to set up a new industrial estate at Dunton End. The new estate will occupy the land behind the Dunton End housing estate to the west of the River Leaf. The land at present is not in use.

The Dunton End Industrial Estate will be for light industry such as clothing, electronics, household appliances and so on. Tronny Ltd, the makers of hi-fi equipment, Kiddigear Ltd and Ladda-craft may be interested in setting up new factories there.

Comprehension

1 What kinds of buildings do you usually find on a housing estate?
2 What kinds of buildings do you usually find on an industrial estate?
3 What kinds of things does light industry make? (The news item mentions three of them. Think of some others.
4 What kinds of things do you think Kiddigear makes? (Guess. What other way is there of saying 'gear' for 'kids'?)
5 What sort of things do you think Laddacraft make? (A clue. They make 'household appliances'. What kind?)

 **page 26**

Letters to a newspaper

These two letters to the editor appeared in the local paper, *The Marbury Post*, the week after the article appeared. The first one is against the idea of a new industrial estate:

The second letter agreed with the idea of a new industrial estate. Here it is:

> Your article last week states that the land behind the Dunton End housing estate is not in use and you are quite wrong. Football teams use one of the fields. Children from the estate play on the waste land. They have played there for years. We can't let planners ruin all that. The new industrial estate must go somewhere else. We don't want it at Dunton End. It must be stopped.
>
> Judith Hallworth (Mrs)

> It was splendid to read the good news in last week's paper. The new industrial estate at Dunton End will be the best thing that has happened to this town in years. Many of the unemployed in Marbury must have read the news item with pleasure and with hope.
>
> The new industrial estate will not mean jobs for everyone. Our problems are too great to be solved in one stroke. But the new industries will bring work and new life for many. Let us all pull together so that it may be built as soon as possible.
>
> H. J. Peterson

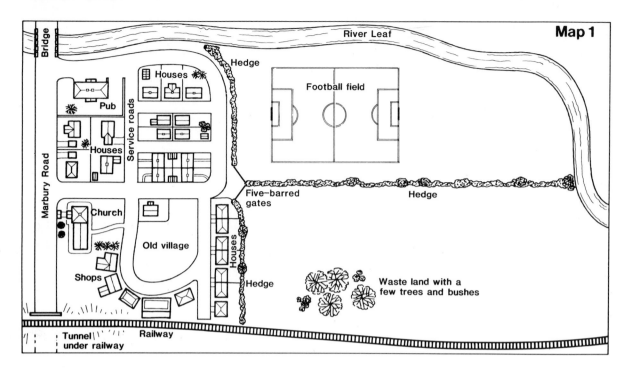

Questions on map one

■ Answer the questions after you have studied this map.

1 Is the pub near the river or near the railway?
2 Is the football field nearer the river or nearer the railway?
3 How does the Marbury Road cross the river?
4 How does it cross the railway?
5 How do you get into the fields from the estate?
6 What large building is about half-way along the Marbury Road between the railway and the river?
7 If you come into the estate from the Marbury Road, do you turn right or left to get to the shops? (Think about this one. Try turning the map sideways. Then you are looking at it as if you were on the Marbury Road.)

 page 33

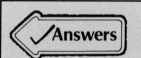 *Questions on page 25*

1 On a housing estate you usually find houses, flats, a pub or pubs, a car park and shops.
2 On an industrial estate you usually find factories where people work and car parks.
3 Three things are mentioned in the news item. Light industry makes clothing, electronic equipment and household appliances.
4 Kiddigear make clothing for children.
5 Laddacraft make small step ladders for use in the home. (They also make ironing boards but you would have to be a genius to have guessed that.)

You might have other ideas and have given different answers. Discuss these as a class.

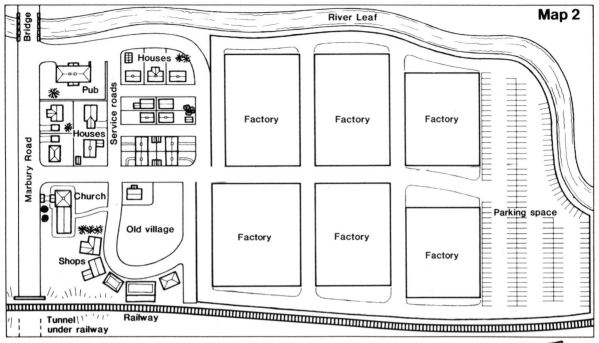

Map 2

Compare two maps

Here is a map of Dunton End with the proposed new industrial estate. Compare Map 2 with Map 1 on page 26 and look at the amount of space the factories take up. Note the kind of land that is going to be taken up by these factories. Then read the section called 'The People of Marbury'.

The people of Marbury

There were many more letters to the *Marbury Post* about the new industrial estate. Some were in favour of it and some were not. People took sides and feelings were strong. Here are some of the people involved. Against their names are the reasons why they feel as they do:

Those FOR the new industrial estate

Mrs Marion Evans

She is the Assistant Planning Officer. She has been round all the businesses in the town and found that they are nearly all very much in favour of the industrial estate. Two of these businesses will set up new factories there. She has also been in contact with other businesses in other parts of the country. She has the names of several who may set up factories on the new estate.

Mr G F Gordon

He is a Government official and he deals with unemployment. He has set up several of these new industrial estates in other parts of the country and he feels they have been a success and brought work and money to people who needed these things.

Miss Bella Quarry

She is a union official. She represents women who work in factories where there is light industry. Her members in the union in Marbury can see that jobs at present in the town are getting fewer and fewer. They would be very pleased to be able to find jobs on the industrial estate.

Mr E Braithwaite

He has been out of work for six months. He hopes to find a job in the electronics factory and he is only one of several men like himself on the housing estate.

Mr H J Peterson

He is a builder who lives on the housing estate. He is having a hard time. He hopes for work from the building of the industrial estate and makes no secret of this.

Miss Sitai Desai

She keeps one of the shops on the housing estate. She and two other shopkeepers welcome the new industrial estate. They think it will bring them business.

Those AGAINST the new industrial estate

Mr E Walker

He is the Chief Fire Officer at the Marbury Road Fire Station. He is worried about dealing with fires on the industrial estate. There may be problems. It is well off the main road. Fire engines may have difficulty in getting there if there are a lot of parked cars on the housing estate.

Mrs H Gold

She speaks for the Local History Society. She has heard that the road into the new industrial estate will have to be widened, where it meets the main Marbury Road. This will mean that the beautiful old houses from the old village will have to come down. This will be a tragedy.

Mrs Judith Hallworth

There are many women on the housing estate who feel as she does. Children have played happily on the waste land since the housing estate was built. If that goes, they will have to play on the roads. With heavy lorries going in and out, this will be very dangerous.

Mr I Smith

He is President of the Wildlife Society. All the wild life—including some quite rare birds—that live on the waste land will disappear.

Mr P Bradley

He speaks for the Dunton End football and cricket teams. They have nowhere else to play their matches. They have spent money on a hut where players can change. All their efforts over many years will be wasted.

Miss E Glenn

She will be living right next to the new industrial estate. She represents a lot of old people living in the houses near where the factories will be built. The noise will be very disturbing.

Writing a speech or a letter

■ Choose one name from the first list and one from the second. Then write a short speech – or a letter to the newspaper – as if you are that person. First write as if you are in favour of a new industrial estate. Then write as if you are strongly against it.

Begin your letter to the newspaper 'Dear Sir,' and end it 'Yours faithfully' (with a small 'f' at the beginning of 'faithfully'). Set out the letter properly with your address at the top.

A public meeting

There is a public meeting to discuss whether the new industrial estate should be built or not. Some of the people in the lists are there. People will state their arguments for or against the estate.

■ Choose a person from the list. Then think about that person. Write a few notes on him or her on the following points:

1 Is he or she young or old?
2 Is he or she a shy or talkative person?
3 Is he or she a determined person?
4 Is he or she a reasonable person? Or does that person get angry, if people disagree with him or her?
5 Would he or she change his or her views, if strong arguments were brought against them?
6 What kind of points would that person bring up at the meeting?

■ Some of the points to be made by each person are given in the lists. Think up more details to go with these points.
Refer to the maps to help make your points.

■ Then write a full account of that person.

■ Invent other people who would be for or against the industrial estate and add them to the lists.

■ Act out the meeting as a group. Argue the case for and against the new industrial estate. Only one person should speak at a time and each person should speak at least once.
You need a Chairperson. He or she must say who is allowed to speak next and everyone must obey the Chairperson.
   At the end take a vote for or against the idea of a new industrial estate.

■ Read the following passages and then answer the questions.

A Town

The main road to the coast takes most of the traffic away from the centre of town. Turn off this road and you come to the main street where there are no big shops, although there is a bank on the corner and a bread and cake shop opposite that. Next to the bank is a shop that sells ice-cream and sweets which has space invader machines as well so that it is always fairly full of young people. As you go up the left-hand side of the street you pass a grocer's, a newsagent's, an electrical shop, a shop selling camping equipment and a plumber's.

On the right-hand side of the street there are two chemists, the Post Office, the library, another bank, a greengrocer's and two shoe shops.

It is a small, rather sleepy town but it does have the ruins of a castle and an old railway station with steam trains and a small museum, all of which can be visited.

There are tennis courts, playing fields, a park and a swimming bath. The town has a cinema and sometimes plays are put on in the Memorial Hall.

Comprehension

1 Why is there not much traffic in the centre of this town?
2 Why is the shop that sells ice-cream and sweets usually full?
3 How many chemists are there in the street?
4 Name two of the places that might be interesting to visit.
5 What games could you play or what could you do if you wanted to be energetic?

 **page 33**

Dusk

On an autumn evening the town is full of whispers. In that small, out-of-the way place there are never many people about and there is not much traffic. The houses and shops in the main street seem to huddle closer together as darkness falls. When all the shops are closed and everyone has gone home the sound of footsteps rings out and echoes among the narrow alleys.

Later, and especially on a cloudy night, the shadows between the street lamps shift and change as if they were alive. The lamp outside the church shines palely, throwing the churchyard beyond into deep gloom. On a windy night, the dim, black shapes of the trees among the gravestones seem to dance and beckon.

Comprehension

1 What is the town full of on an autumn evening?
2 What do the houses and shops in the main street seem to do?
3 How do footsteps sound when the streets are empty?
4 What do the shadows between the street lamps look like at night?
5 What do the trees in the graveyard do when it is windy?

Comparing the passages

Which of the passages, 'A Town' or 'Dusk', gives you more facts about the town?
Which of the two passages tells you more about how the writer feels about the place?

 **Answers** page 36

Writing about a place

The short passage 'A Town' gave you the facts about the town. The passage 'Dusk' told you more how the person writing felt about a town.

In the following suggestions, numbers 1 and 3 ask you to give facts about a place. Numbers 2 and 4 ask you about how you feel about a place.

■ Choose one of these and write about it.

1 Write about a place you know in a town or a village or a city and give as many *facts* as you can about it. Does it have shops, buildings of interest, interesting places to visit?

2 Write about a place you know in a town or village or city but do not give too many facts about it. Try to show how you *feel* about the place.

3 You have the power to pull down buildings and put up new ones. You can even alter roads. You can build football grounds, swimming baths, speedways or anything you like. What changes would you make in your home town? Write about them.

4 Is there a particular place such as a wood or a lake in the country or a park or building or shopping centre in a town that you like? Write a description of it, saying why you like it.

 *Questions on page 26*

1 The pub is near the river.
2 The football field is nearer the river.
3 The Marbury Road goes over the river by way of a bridge.
4 It goes under the railway in a tunnel.
5 You get into the fields by way of a five-barred gate.
6 The large building in that position is the church.
7 You turn right.

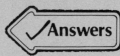 *Questions on page 31*

1 The road to the coast takes most of the traffic away from the centre of town.
2 It has space invader machines in it.
3 There are two chemists.
4 You could visit the ruins of the castle or the old railway station or the small museum. (If you have named two of these, you are right.)
5 You could play tennis on the courts or football or cricket and other games on the playing fields or you could go swimming in the baths.

Describing people from pictures

■ Look at the two groups of pictures and the people in them. Choose one person from each group. Answer these questions about them.

What are the names of your two people?

How old are they?

Where do they live? In a flat or in a house?

If they live in a house, is it in a terrace or is it semi-detached or detached?

Is the house in this country? Is it in the centre of town? Is it in a suburb?

Is it near a park or a shopping centre?

How does the person usually travel about? By car? By bike or motor-bike? By bus or train?

What kind of work does the person do? Does he or she like the job?

What does the person do if he or she wants to enjoy him or herself?

Does the person have strong likes or dislikes? What are they?

Finally think up an unusual hobby or interest each of your people might have.

Group A

Group B

■ Use your answers to write as full an account as you can of *one* of the people you have chosen.

Giving a talk

Here are parts of three talks given by three different people.

A Horseriding

You have to have a field to put your horse in. That can be quite expensive. I don't know how much because my uncle lets me have his free. I have to collect the eggs his hens lay in return. And then of course there's hay. If you want to go in for jumping competitions you have to be quite good. Some of the fences are very high.

On the other hand if you're a beginner you can start in the novices' group. You need to keep your horse inside in the winter and that can be expensive. My dad is always complaining how much the stable costs. If you go in for a competition, make sure you've groomed your horse well. It takes a long time to do it properly. Then, of course, there's mucking out the stables in the winter. That's hard work and you need the right clothes. That reminds me.

When you groom your horse for a competition you need the right implements. I'm not sure what they are called, because my uncle bought them for me. My dad had to pay, though. There's a thing like a big comb. You need to know your horse well before you try jumping. Always give him some encouragement if he does it right.

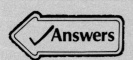 **Answers** *Questions on page 32*

1 It is full of whispers.
2 They seem to huddle closer together.
3 The footsteps ring out and echo.
4 The shadows shift and change as if they were alive.
5 They seem to dance and beckon.

B Owning a motor bike

If you are really keen on killing yourself, here are three ways to do it. Don't wear a crash helmet. It's against the law, of course, so if you're lucky you'll be stopped by the police and fined or even banned from riding. If you're not lucky, it won't be long before you have an accident. If it is a minor one, such as slipping off on an icy or wet road, you may escape with a head injury. If it is a major accident, you'll become a statistic on a police report, adding one to the total of motor cyclists' deaths.

Weaving in and out of slow-moving traffic is another way to kill yourself. Many riders think that as they are not as wide as cars, they can escape traffic jams by nipping round the side of slow-moving or stationary cars. I had a friend who did this—until a car driver opened his door to see what was causing the hold-up. My friend was lucky. He only had a broken collarbone. He could have had a broken neck.

The third way to kill yourself is seeing how fast you can go, preferably racing someone up a motorway. There are many motorcyclists who have boasted about how far they can get in half an hour—some of them have only got six feet—under the ground!

I have here the police statistics for road deaths and injuries in this county for last year.

Three pedal cyclists were killed, thirty-seven car drivers and sixty-four motorcyclists. And if you think there are nearly as many car drivers as motorcyclists killed, then remember how many more cars than motorbikes there are on the road—in proportion to these numbers there are ten times as many motorcyclists as car drivers killed.

C Oliver Cromwell

Oliver Cromwell was born in Huntingdon on 25th April 1599 and for nigh on thirty years lived a life in no way more remarkable than those of contemporaries in his own walk of life. He married Elizabeth Bourchier in 1620 and raised a numerous brood. In 1629 he was elected to the Parliament of King Charles I as member for Huntingdon.

Comprehension

1 Which speech has been copied word for word from a book?
2 Which speech has no organisation, and jumps from one point to the next without any connection?
3 Which speaker has looked up facts to help illustrate the speech?
4 Which speaker ought to have found out some facts, but hasn't? Which facts are they?
5 Which speaker has organised the speech so that one point is well-connected to the next?
6 Which speaker has used long-winded words that he probably doesn't understand?
7 Which speaker tells you details that are nothing to do with the subject? Which details are these?

 ✓Answers > **page 39**

Tips for making a speech

1 Choose a subject you are interested in and know thoroughly. Then you will be able to illustrate from your experience as B has.

2 Look up any important details that you don't know. Illustrate your talk with a diagram or a drawing, if it will help. Put it on the blackboard *before* your talk.

3 Make notes on the important points. You should refer to them throughout your speech and so will avoid the muddle of A. Notes should not be chunks of your speech. If you read your speech you will not be able to look at your audience.

Here are the notes for the whole of B's speech:

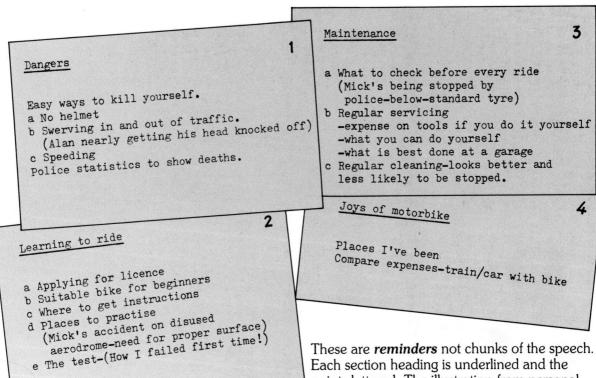

Dangers   1

Easy ways to kill yourself.
a No helmet
b Swerving in and out of traffic.
  (Alan nearly getting his head knocked off)
c Speeding
Police statistics to show deaths.

Learning to ride   2

a Applying for licence
b Suitable bike for beginners
c Where to get instructions
d Places to practise
  (Mick's accident on disused
  aerodrome-need for proper surface)
e The test-(How I failed first time!)

Maintenance   3

a What to check before every ride
  (Mick's being stopped by
  police-below-standard tyre)
b Regular servicing
  -expense on tools if you do it yourself
  -what you can do yourself
  -what is best done at a garage
c Regular cleaning-looks better and
  less likely to be stopped.

Joys of motorbike   4

Places I've been
Compare expenses-train/car with bike

These are **reminders** not chunks of the speech. Each section heading is underlined and the points lettered. The illustration from personal experience is put in brackets. The illustration is closely connected with the point.

■ Now prepare notes for a talk and give it to the class. Choose a subject that really interests you. Look up the necessary facts and make orderly notes, as B has done.

Revision and further work

■ You have been asked to give a talk. You like dogs and have decided to give your talk on keeping one as a pet. These are your ideas:

Care of health and amount of exercise
Feeding it when young
Advantages and drawbacks of keeping a dog as a pet
Choosing a dog as a pet
What it eats and how to feed it
Training the pet
Care of health when young

Now you have to put these ideas in order. Write out the ideas again, putting them in order so that one idea leads to another.

■ You and your uncle ran a disco for charity in a local hall. It went very well. People were well behaved. It ended at eleven and raised a fair amount of money for charity. But a letter has appeared in your local paper complaining bitterly that it was very rowdy, that there were fights outside and that it went on until early morning.

    Your uncle is away travelling. It is up to you to write a letter to the paper to answer the complaint and to say what really happened.
Set out your letter properly, beginning 'Dear Sir,' and ending 'Yours faithfully'. Do not attack the person who complained. Your letter will have more effect if your tone is reasonable and persuasive.

■ Here are five sentences. Write them out, putting in the capitals and full stops.

it was a very old car he painted the picture on the wall two swordsmen fought bravely on the field of Waterloo bridge the gap with a chocolate snack

■ Write out each of the following sentences twice. Each time match the verb with the right words at the end of the sentence. Use a dictionary to help you.

a The cat spat/purred at him ferociously/in a friendly way.
b The soldier sank/hurled himself to the ground exhaustedly/frantically.
c She called to/screamed at her little brother teasingly/furiously.
d She danced/stumbled across the stage drunkenly/elegantly.

■ What is wrong with the following? Write them out correctly.

morton street   mr john wilson   frank slater

mrs yasmin patel   london road

the dunton   end industrial estate

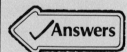 **Answers**   *Questions on page 37*

1 C
2 A
3 B
4 A She should have found out the cost of renting a field and the correct names for the implements needed to groom a horse.
5 B
6 C
7 A She has to collect the eggs to get the field rent-free.
Her uncle bought the grooming implements but her father paid him for them.

3 Who says what – speech punctuation

Mrs Gregg runs the Post Office and grocery shop in the village of Harton. Joan Pearson helps her. It is about ten o'clock in the morning and the shop is empty of customers. Mrs Gregg and Joan are chatting together behind the counter. Suddenly Mick Brent and Ted Lawson come in. Both men are wearing stocking masks and Mick is carrying a shot-gun. This is how the conversation starts. Both men and women say something. But who says what?

Don't move. And keep your hands on the counter. You won't get away with this. Shut up and stand still. You daren't use that gun. Try me. Open the till.

It's not easy, is it? You probably worked out what the women said and what the two robbers said. But was it Joan or Mrs Gregg who said, 'You won't get away with this'?

Setting out speech

When writing a play or writing speech, you give each new speaker a new line, like this:

Mick: Don't move.
Ted: And keep your hands on the counter.
Mrs Gregg: You won't get away with this.
Ted: Shut up and stand still.
Joan: You daren't use that gun.
Mick   Try me.
Ted: Open the till.

Writing it like this makes it much easier to follow. Jokes and riddles are easier to read – and funnier – if each speaker is given a separate line. Here are two jokes and one riddle. Write them out properly, starting each speech on a new line.

Man at the top of Blackpool Tower: It's a long way down to the ground. Do people fall off here very often? His Friend: No. Only once. George: Why do hens have short legs? Bill: If they had long ones their eggs would get smashed by the fall. Kevin: What makes a good parting gift? Ann: A comb.

Writing your own jokes

■ Write out some of your own jokes in this way. Notice how each speech begins with a capital and ends with a full-stop or a question mark. Watch for the question mark!

Jumbled jokes

■ Unjumble these jokes and set them out correctly:
The outside man is invisible Butler:

him Tell I him can't Lord: see
Mini do you get How elephants into four a Gill: I John: know don't

Two Gill: back two front the in and two the is worse apple while it eating you are maggot a What finding than an in Jane:

maggot Finding a half Sarah:

 **page 50**

The Spennymoor Scraping

This is from a short story called 'The Spennymoor Scraping' in a book, *One of the Gang*, by Dick Cate. A thirteen-year-old boy is talking about his father.

Part 1

My dad was a clever-clogs. There was no doubt about that. He could recite whole poems that he'd learnt by heart when he was at school and he was always writing down the words of Geordie songs on the back of envelopes and then singing them up at the Workman's Club where he got free dockets for beer. We had loads of books in the cupboard under the stairs that he'd won with *John Bull Bullets*, and if he sent a poem to *The Northern Echo* they were sure to publish it and send him a ten-bob note.

But he wasn't soft. He knocked about with a chap called Andrew Dunlevy and when they were young they used to bite the tops off beer bottles with their teeth (that's why they both had false ones now).

No, he wasn't soft. Except about one thing. Khaki Campbells. Ducks.

I'll tell you a story about him. One year we were going to have a duck for Christmas—we usually had a chicken. So my dad bought one and kept it all through the summer. Then when it came time to cook it, my mam sent him over to the hen run to kill it.

He was away for a long time.

Comprehension

1 What payment did the boy's father get for singing at the club?
2 What did the family usually have for Christmas?
3 Who went out to kill the duck?
4 What evidence does the boy give to show that he thought his father was a 'clever-clogs'?
5 What do you think *The Northern Echo* was?

Part 2

'What on earth's happened to your father?' my mam asked. 'If he doesn't get a move on, it'll be too late to have that duck for Christmas!'

When he came in he didn't have the duck with him. He went straight to his chair by the fire and lit his pipe up. He didn't say a word.

'Where's the duck?' said my mother.

He didn't answer. He just kept looking at the fire. He often did that. He went off in a sort of dream.

'Where's the duck?' said my mother again.

'I haven't got it,' he said.

'I can see that,' said my mother. 'Where is it?'

'In the hen run,' he said.

'What do you mean – "in the hen run"?'

'What I say,' he said. 'It's in the hen run.'

'Well, I don't know whether it's me that's daft or you,' said my mother.

My dad didn't answer.

'Well, are we going to have that duck for Christmas or are we not?' asked my mother.

'No,' said my dad. 'We're not.'

'Well, I don't know what we are going to eat,' said my mother, 'because I haven't a bit of butcher's meat in the house!'

'We'll have a chicken,' said my dad.

'We've had a chicken for Christmas ever since I came to this house,' said my mother, 'and I'm just pig-sick of them. *I* thought we were going to have a duck this Christmas.'

'Well, you know what thought did,' he said.

And that was the end of the matter.

Comprehension

6 Who was annoyed about not having the duck for Christmas?

7 Who was the most soft-hearted, the boy's mother or his father? Why do you think so?

Part 3

Mind you, I could see my mam's point of view, because we'd fed that duck on all the tasty morsels for the best part of a year. On the other hand, though, I could see my dad's point of view. That Khaki Campbell had become a sort of pet. It even had a nickname. We called it Donald, and when you went into the run it didn't run away like the hens did but came quacking up to you, like a little old man, and as trustful as anything—or, at least, that was the impression it managed to give. Maybe that duck, for all its daft look, was cleverer than any of us thought.

At any rate, we didn't eat it, not that Christmas or any other. It waddled on for years and years until it finally dropped down dead, probably from over-feeding. We buried it under the apple tree next to my rabbits and mice and a tortoise we once had.

And that's what I mean about my dad being soft about Khaki Campbells.

from *The Spennymoor Scraping* by Dick Cate

Comprehension

8 What was the name of the duck?
9 What did it usually do when you went into the hen run?
10 How did the duck die in the end?
11 Why did the boy think that the duck might have been clever?
12 How do you know that the boy had had other pets?
13 What evidence is there that he might not have been very good at looking after them?

Check your answers to all three parts with those on page 50.

Speech marks

■ Look at the conversation in the story again and answer these questions.

1 How are the speeches set out to show a new speaker each time?
2 What marks come at the beginning and end of each speech?
3 Which punctuation marks come just inside these marks? (There are four of them.)

Speech punctuation

■ Now practise speech punctuation step by step.

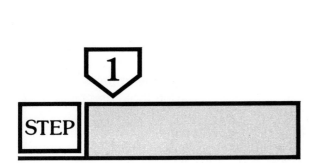

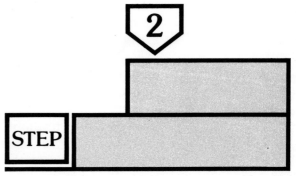

Give a new line for each speaker.
Write double inverted commas (like this ". . . .") round each speech. Write a full stop after each speech **inside** the inverted commas like this:

> "I'm going to the disco tonight."
> "I'll come with you."

■ Write out the following speeches, setting them out and punctuating them correctly.

1 You need a hair cut   I know
2 I've got something in my eye   Let me have a look
3 I like that necklace you're wearing   I bought it on holiday

When you add the words to show who is speaking, you put a comma inside the inverted commas and not a full stop, like this:

> "In the hen run," he said.

Notice that you put the full stop after **said.**

In the following:

> *Give a new line for each speaker:*
> *Put inverted commas round each speech.*
> *Put a comma inside the inverted commas.*
> *Put a full stop at the end of each line.*

4 I can give you a pound she said I need more than that he said
5 We'll wait for you outside the bus station she said I won't be late he said
6 Your hair looks nice Linda said I set it myself last night Stella told her

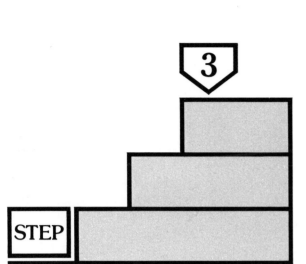

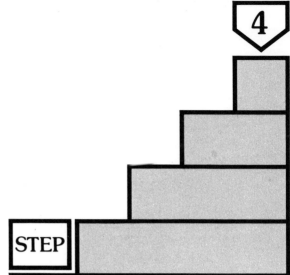

When a speaker asks a question, you put a question mark inside the inverted commas, like this:

"Where's the duck?" said my mother.

If you put a question mark, you do not need a comma, as well.

In the following:

Give a new line for each speaker.
Put in the inverted commas.
Put a comma or question mark and full stops where needed.

7 When will I see you again asked Gran   I'll come over next Saturday Vikki told her
8 How can I get this mud off my jacket Leroy asked   Wait till it dries and then brush it off said his mother
9 What are you doing tomorrow asked Sabir   I'm helping my father in the shop said Sita

If a speaker shouts or exclaims, you put an exclamation mark inside the inverted commas, like this

"Look out!" he yelled.

Notice that you **don't put a comma with the exclamation mark.**

In the following:

Give a new line for each speaker
Put in the inverted commas.
Put in the commas, exclamation marks and full stops where needed.

10 What a beautiful sari Eleni exclaimed   I got it in Bombay Leela told her
11 Stop Ian shouted to the bus driver   He didn't hear you Susan said gloomily
12 I'm drowning he screamed   That water's only a foot deep Errol told him.
13 Goal he yelled   It was offside, you nit said his sister

 **page 50**

47

Writing ideas

■ Choose one of these ideas and write out the conversation the people might have. Invent names for the people speaking.

1 Three of you are planning a holiday. Is it a walking holiday or a cycling holiday or a trip by train to a camp or hostel or camp site? What are you going to take with you? Swimming things? Clothes to wear at a disco?

Two of you have fairly sensible ideas. The third person has never been away before and keeps asking obvious, sometimes stupid questions. Do you get annoyed with him or her or do you sort it all out in a friendly manner in the end?

2 A girl wants to go out in the evening. Her parents want her to stay in. They don't like the place she wants to go to and they don't like the people she will be with.

You will have to decide what their reasons are. You will also have to decide what sort of arguments the girl gives for going out. Does she persuade her parents to let her go or not?

3 The three old people in the picture below are talking about the old days. They talk about what they did when they were young and the way in which people's behaviour has changed.

Do they all think that times were better in the old days or do one or two of them prefer the present?

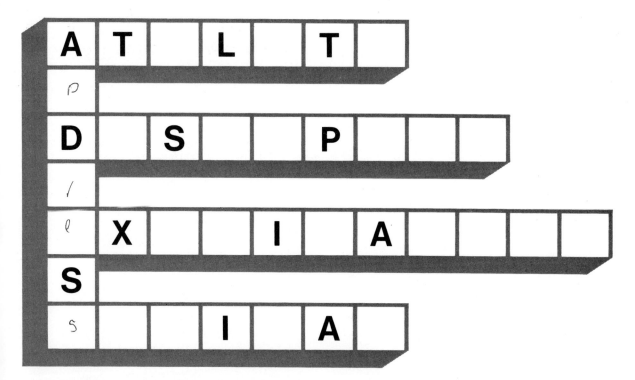

****

Listening test one: The Spectacles

■ Listen to this story (text on page 112) and then write the answers to the following questions.

1 Where had the spectacles been thrown away?
2 When were they found again?
3 How many years is it since they were thrown away?
4 In which town was the rubbish dump?
5 Who provided the money to restore and study the spectacles?
6 Why is their age not in doubt?
7 When was the river wall built?
8 What was the name of the site supervisor?
9 What sort of condition were the spectacles in when they were found?
10 What had happened to the lenses?
11 What material were the frames made from?
12 From what animal had that material come?

Spelling – crossword

Draw this pattern of squares in your book. Make sure you get the right number of squares in each line. Then fill in the missing words. Clues are given below.
Clues

Down
1 What you write on the front of an envelope.

Across
1 A good runner or jumper or javelin thrower is this.
2 If you make something vanish, you make it this.
3 A doctor gives you this or you have one in school.
4 If two things are nearly the same, they are this.

 **Answers** *Questions on page 41*

Man at the top of Blackpool Tower:
It's a long way to the ground.
Do people fall off here very often?
His Friend: No. Only once.

George: Why do hens have such short legs?
Bill: If they had long ones their eggs would get smashed in the fall.

Kevin: What makes a good parting gift?
Ann: A comb.

 **Answers** *Questions on pages 43, 44 and 45*

1 The boy's father got paid in free dockets for beer.
2 They usually had a chicken.
3 The father went out to kill the duck.
4 He could recite poems that he'd learnt at school and sing Geordie songs.
5 It was a newspaper.
6 The boy's mother was annoyed.
7 The boy's father was the most soft-hearted because he couldn't kill the duck.
8 The duck was called 'Donald'.
9 It came quacking up to you like a little old man.
10 It probably died from over-feeding.
11 It always came up to people in a friendly way.
12 He had buried rabbits and mice and a tortoise in the garden.
13 They had all died.

 **Answers** *Questions on page 45*

1 Each new speaker is given a new line.
2 Inverted commas are put at the beginning and end of each speech.
3 You should have found commas(,), full stops (.), exclamation marks (!) and question marks (?) inside the inverted commas.

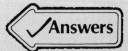 **Answers** *Questions on pages 46 and 47*

1 "You need a hair cut." "I know."
2 "I've got something in my eye."
"Let me have a look."
3 "I like that necklace you're wearing."
"I bought it on holiday."
4 "I can give you a pound," she said.
"I need more than that," he said.
5 "We'll wait for you outside the bus station," she said.
"I won't be late," he said.
6 "Your hair looks nice," Linda said.
"I set it myself last night," Stella told her.
7 "When will I see you again?" asked Gran.
"I'll come over next Saturday," Vikki told her.
8 "How can I get his mud off my jacket?" Leroy asked.
"Wait until it dries and then brush it off," said his mother.
9 "What are you doing tomorrow?" asked Sabir.
"I'm helping my father in the shop," said Sita.
10 'What a beautiful sari!" Eleni exclaimed.
"I got it in Bombay," Leela told her.
11 "Stop!" Ian shouted to the bus driver.
"He didn't hear you," Susan said gloomily.
12 "I'm drowning!" he yelled.
"That water's only a foot deep," Errol told him.
13 "Goal!" he yelled.
"It was offside, you nit," said his sister.

Revision and further work

- Complete these sentences.

1 If you help me to get the dinner ready, I'll
. . . .
2 Though she hadn't seen him for years, she
. . . .
3 Unless they hear from him tomorrow, they
will . . . .
4 Before she went to school in the morning,
she . . .
5 Until he found the key, he . . .

- Write out the following, putting in all the speech punctuation correctly.

I want twelve pounds, Dad said Peter Twelve pounds What for said his father To go to Longsands Peter told him Well, you can't have it this week his father said But I've got to have it Peter insisted

- In the following conversation, four question marks, one exclamation mark, several commas and full stops are missing. Write it out, punctuating it correctly. Don't forget to *put each speech on a new line.*

> What's the number of the house said Martin I don't know Jean told him Who's going to be at the party asked Pak We aren't, if we can't find the house grumbled Errol Listen Martin exclaimed You've got it. man Errol said How do you know that's the right house asked Jean Can't you hear the music said Pak

The printer has used single inverted commas, like this '. . . .'. In printed books, speech is usually enclosed in single inverted commas. When *you* are writing speech, however, *you should use double inverted commas, like this* ". . . ."

4 Survival English – chemicals

The Chemist's Shop

Jayne always liked the chemist's shop. There was a warm, pinky glow from the lighting. There was the smell of perfumes; and there were the colours of the different packages and glowing glass bottles. She felt comfortable in there. It was so different from the noisy supermarket.

She always had an urge to buy things in there. She did not feel this in any other shop. She seemed to want Horlicks tablets; a new lip salve; sun-glasses and some lavender soap.

There were bowls of mixed goods on offer which stood like bran tubs. She longed to have a good rummage in them and come up with a treasure. At the back of the bowls were stands and racks of toothbrushes, razors, films, Elastoplast, and all manner of things for the feet.

The centrepiece of the shop was a glass case which contained gold and silver topped perfumes which did not have prices on. She had never dared to ask the price as her Mum had said they were so expensive. There was an Eastern mystery about them.

There was obviously not enough space on the glass shelves or on the crowded counter because some goods were piled up on the floor looking ready to topple over: tissue boxes; toilet rolls; bottles of Lucozade.

Presiding over this Aladdin's cave was the chemist himself, Mr Atkins. He was dressed in a crisp, white coat and looked like an advert for a washing powder. He had thick glasses and a slight stoop from bending over for many years to fill bottles with medicine and to count tablets in containers.

Comprehension

■ Write the answers to these questions:

1 List the things mentioned that Jayne saw in the chemist's shop.
2 List some other things she might have mentioned. Star any that you think contain chemicals.
3 What did she like about the chemist's shop?
4 Which is your favourite shop? Why?
5 Why do shops use lighting in the daytime?
6 Why do some shops play music?
7 What three items begin with capital letters? Why?
8 Why did the perfume bottles have gold and silver tops?
9 Why is the shop called 'an Aladdin's cave'?
10 What is another name for chemist? It begins : phar . . . .

■ How does the writer of this piece build up his picture of the chemist's shop? Which of your five senses does it appeal to?

The language of the chemist

Chemicals are packaged attractively. They look so harmless that we do not always realise that they must be treated with great care. Where children are, extreme caution must be taken even with things like powdered milk. Look at the labels and instructions on the following pages. Then answer the questions on them. You may need to use a dictionary.

THE TABLETS

to be taken

three times a day

Keep out of children's reach

CALVERTS (GRANTHAM) LTD.
Dispensing Chemists
23b St. Peter's Hill, GRANTHAM
Tel. 3062

1 What *two* things does this label tell you to do?

POISON

NOT TO BE TAKEN

2 What must you not do with this medicine?

**KEEP OUT OF
THE REACH
OF CHILDREN**

3 Where would you put tablets in your house to obey this label?

CAUTION: This may cause drowsiness. If affected, do not drive, or operate machinery.

4 What does drowsiness mean? What must you not do if you become drowsy after taking the tablets?

POISON—FOR ANIMAL TREATMENT ONLY

5 Is this medicine suitable for human beings?

This is one of....2.............
containers of the **SAME**
preparation. Please use up
the contents of one **BEFORE
STARTING ANOTHER.**

6 When can you open the second container?

These Tablets to be dissolved under the tongue

7 What does dissolved mean?

> **CAUTION.—This preparation may cause serious inflammation of the skin in certain persons and should be used only in accordance with expert advice.**

8   What does inflammation mean? Who might give expert advice?

> **CAUTION.**—THESE EAR DROPS MUST NOT BE DILUTED WITH WATER

9   What does diluted mean?

> **CAUTION.—It is dangerous to take this preparation except under medical supervision.**

10 Who will give you medical supervision?

> CARE SHOULD BE TAKEN TO AVOID CONTAMINATION DURING USE AND EYE DROPS SHOULD BE DISCARDED ONE MONTH AFTER THE CONTAINER IS FIRST OPENED

11 What does contamination mean? What does discarded mean?

> **N.B.:** You require a further supply from us to complete your prescription. Please return this container or Quote Ref. No...364........

12 What must you do to obtain a further prescription?

> **An Antibiotic**
>
> **To the patient**
>
> After mixing keep in a cool place (6-15C) or refrigerator. Shake before using. Discard unused portion ten days after dispensing.

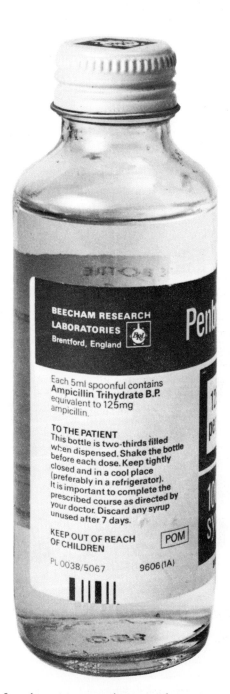

BEECHAM RESEARCH LABORATORIES
Brentford, England

Each 5ml spoonful contains Ampicillin Trihydrate B.P. equivalent to 125mg ampicillin.

TO THE PATIENT
This bottle is two-thirds filled when dispensed. Shake the bottle before each dose. Keep tightly closed and in a cool place (preferably in a refrigerator). It is important to complete the prescribed course as directed by your doctor. Discard any syrup unused after 7 days.

KEEP OUT OF REACH OF CHILDREN   POM

PL 0038/5067   9606 (1A)

13a What are the three instructions given with this antibiotic?

13b In what ways are these antibiotic instructions different?

Anti-histamines (found in travel sickness pills)

> Marzine acts rapidly and will often stop symptoms of travel sickness after they appear.
>
> > **Warning:** May cause drowsiness. If affected do not drive or operate machinery. Avoid alcoholic drink.
>
> Note: Current authoritative opinion is that no medicine should be taken by a pregnant woman, especially during the first four months of pregnancy, unless prescribed by a doctor.

14 What other label is like these instructions? But what does the other one miss out? What must a pregnant woman avoid?

Bran Slim diet plan

> **Warning: Chew thoroughly.** *Do not swallow tablets whole.* Keep out of the reach of children. Not to be used when abdominal pain, nausea, vomiting, or other symptoms of appendicitis are present.

15 Where would you get abdominal pain? What is nausea? What is vomiting?

Sister Laura's food for babies

> **ALWAYS shake the bottle before and during feeding.** Twenty-four hours supply of feeds may be made up at one time and kept in a refrigerator in closed feeding bottles.

16 Why do you think that you have to shake the bottle? What is a closed feeding bottle?

Ostermilk

> ● First wash your hands.
> ● Make sure all utensils are sterilized.
> ● Boil water and allow to cool.
> ● Consult feeding table on pack for quantity of milk required.
> ● Test for temperature by shaking a few drops on inside of wrist. It should be comfortably warm.
>
> **IMPORTANT** – always use one level scoop of powder for each fluid ounce of water.
>
> **REMEMBER! Do not add sugar.** Use only one scoop of powder (4.4g) for each fluid ounce of water. The scoop should not be used for water.

17 What does sterilize mean? What must you not do?

Dinneford's gripe mixture

> Do **not** exceed eight doses in twenty-four hours. If symptoms persist consult your doctor. Do **not** shake. Replace stopper after use.

18 What does 'if symptoms persist' mean?

Delrosa

> **Real Orange Juice and Rose Hip Syrup**
>
> **Always** dilute Delrosa with a minimum of five teaspoons of water to one of Delrosa.
>
> **Never** give a baby a dummy or feeder filled with undiluted fruit syrup.

19 What does 'undiluted' mean?

The language of household products

Not only must we be careful with medicines but also with other chemical products. The average kitchen holds hidden dangers. Look at these labels:

Shift oven cleaner

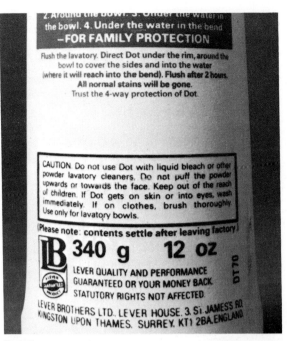

Dot lavatory cleaner

Windolene

Comprehension

1 Each of these products warns about one thing. It is a warning to parents. What is it?
2 What part of the face is particularly vulnerable to chemicals?
3 What advice are you given in the event of an accident to this part of the face?
4 Which product is in a pressurised container?
5 What is another name for this?
6 What must you not do with empty pressurised containers?
7 What is a source of danger on a windowsill or near an oven?
8 What should you do if you swallow any of these products?

Question on the picture

■ Look at this picture. What dangers are there in it?

A pamphlet

■ Now write and design a pamphlet called *Dangers in the Kitchen*.

The Invisible Man

Griffin, after years of research, has found out how to turn things invisible. He has just experimented on a cat successfully. Now he tries it on himself. His landlord, thinking something odd is going on, is trying to eject him from his room:

Part 1

It was all done that evening and night. While I was sitting under the sickly, drowsy influence of the drugs that decolorise blood, there came a repeated knocking at the door. It ceased, footsteps went away and returned, and the knocking was resumed. There was an attempt to push something under the door — a blue paper. Then, in a fit of irritation, I rose, and went and flung the door wide open.

'Now then?' said I.

It was the landlord, with a notice of ejectment or something. He held it out to me, saw something odd about my hands, I expect, and lifted his eyes to my face.

For a moment he gaped. Then he gave a sort of cry, dropped his candle and notice together, and went blundering down the dark passage of the stairs.

I shut the door, locked it, and went to the looking glass. Then I understood his terror. . . . My face was white – like white stone.

Comprehension

1 What does 'drowsy' mean?
2 What do you do if you decolorise something?
3 How do we know the landlord is fussing about?
4 What does 'notice of ejectment' mean?
5 Why does the landlord drop his candle and run off?

Part 2

But it was all horrible. I had not expected the suffering. A night of racking pain, sickness and fainting. I set my teeth, though my skin was presently afire, all my body felt on fire, but I lay there like grim death. I understood how it was that the cat had howled until I put it to sleep. Lucky it was I lived alone and untended in my room. There were times when I sobbed, and groaned, and talked. But I stuck to it. . . . I became unconscious and woke tired in the darkness.

The pain had passed. I thought I was killing myself and I did not care. I shall never forget that dawn, and the strange horror of seeing that my hands had become as clouded glass, and watching them grow clearer and thinner as the day went by, until at last I could see the mess in my room through them, though I closed my transparent eyelids. My limbs became glassy, the bones and the arteries faded, vanished, and the little white nerves went last. I gritted my teeth and stayed there to the end. . . . At last only the dead tips of the finger-nails remained, white, and the brown stain of some acid on my fingers.

I struggled up. At first I was as incapable as a baby – stepping with limbs I could not see. I was weak and very hungry. I went and stared at nothing in my shaving glass – at nothing save where some pigment still remained behind my eyes, fainter than a mist. I had to hang on to the table and press my forehead to the glass.

from *The Invisible Man* by H G Wells

Comprehension

6 What four things make his going invisible horrible?
7 What did his hands look like before they finally disappeared?
8 Which word in the passage means that you can see through something?
9 What went invisible last?
10 Why did Griffin feel 'as incapable as a baby'?

 Now check your answers to both parts with those on page 61.

Discussion or formal debate

■ Discuss the advantages or disadvantages of being invisible.
Organise a formal debate in which some speakers speak for the motion that 'Invisibility would be a good invention' and some speak against it.

Revision and further work

■ Complete the spelling of these words. They have all been used in this section:

chemic . . s   cont . . ner   med . cine

infla . . ation   prep . . ation   di . . olved

dan . . rous   pre . . ription   p . ysician

pr . scribed   refri . . rator   s . mpto . s

temper . ture   ster . li . ed   undil . ted

antib . . tic   ir . . tant   lav . t . ry

inv . s . ble

■ Make a list of any new words you have learned in this section.

■ Find ten verbs in *The Invisible Man* passage.

■ Invent labels and instructions for:

some new cough sweets
a new spot remover
slimming biscuits
a new cleaning spray

Use any of the new words you have learned and discuss your answers.

■ Write a letter to your grandma or a friend explaining what happened to the baby in the kitchen while your mother answered the door.

■ From your imagination write a more detailed description of Mr Atkins the chemist or describe the chemist in your local shop.

■ Imagine a parent has become invisible.
Write a story in which you explain it to visitors or the press.
or Write a story about a football team that had an invisible forward.
or Write a story about a friend who becomes invisible during a science lesson.

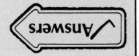

Answers

Questions on pages 59 and 60

1 'Drowsy' means sleepy.
2 You remove the colour from it.
3 He knocks on the door and then stops. He goes away and comes back. He attempts to push a notice under the door.
4 A piece of paper telling someone to leave the house.
5 He sees something odd about Griffin's hands. He sees his very white face.
6 He feels: racking pain sickness faint as if his skin was on fire
7 They look like clouded glass.
8 The word is 'transparent'. Score also for 'glassy'.
9 His finger-nail tips were the last to go invisible.
10 He could not see his feet and he felt like a baby learning to walk for the first time.

61

5 Giving instructions and directions

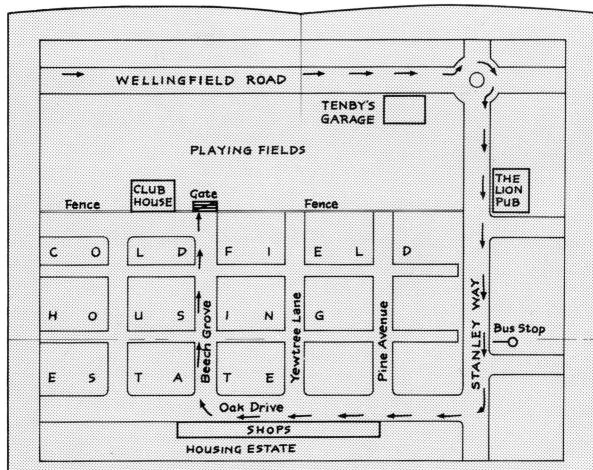

Come in on the Wellingfield Road and turn right at the roundabout. There is a garage and filling station just before the roundabout. It is called Tenby's and it sells BP. After you have turned right at the roundabout, you are going down Stanley Way. On your left you pass a pub called 'The Lion' and then a bus stop. Just after the bus stop you turn right into Oak Drive, with a block of shops ahead of you on your left. Take the third turn on your right, passing Pine Avenue and Yewtree Lane, so that you turn into Beech Grove. The gate, which is marked on the map and leads into the Playing Fields, is right at the end of Beech Grove. The Club House is on your left.

Coldfield Club

Here is a map showing Coldfield Hockey Club's playing ground:

The Coldfield Club's next match was with Moortown. The Coldfield secretary had known visiting clubs to get lost before. So, the previous weekend, he sent the map to Moortown Club and these directions with it. There are several things to notice about these directions.

1 They mention certain things that are easily seen and recognised.
2 The directions give the street names.
3 The directions tell you where the turns are.

Giving the right directions

■ Now use the map to give the right directions for these.

1 You are standing near the gate at the end of Beech Grove.
A man comes across the playing fields and asks you the way to the bus stop in Stanley Way.
He won't, of course, be able to see it because of all the houses in the way.
Write down the directions for getting there. Don't forget to keep turning the map so that you are facing the direction in which he will be going. That way, you should describe the right and left turns correctly. When you have written it, check with someone that you have given correct directions.

2 You are at the end of Yewtree Lane, near the fence.
A woman with a car comes up. She points across the playing fields to Tenby's Garage and asks you how to reach it.
Write the directions for her.
Give the right turns and the left turns correctly, turning the map when you need to.
Then check again with someone that you have all the directions correct.

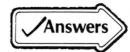 page 67

Spelling – missing letters

■ In the following **bold** words all the vowels (the letters a e i o u) are missing. Clues are given for each word. Write the words out correctly. They have all appeared already in this chapter.

a person who writes letters and looks after the affairs of a club is the **scrtry** (3 letters missing)

a circle where three or more roads meet in the middle of the road is a **rndbt** (5 letters missing)

a number of things are **svrl** (3 letters missing)

When you see a person and realize that you know him or her, he or she is someone you have **rcgnzd** (4 letters missing)

Now check with your dictionary to see that you have all the vowels in their right places.

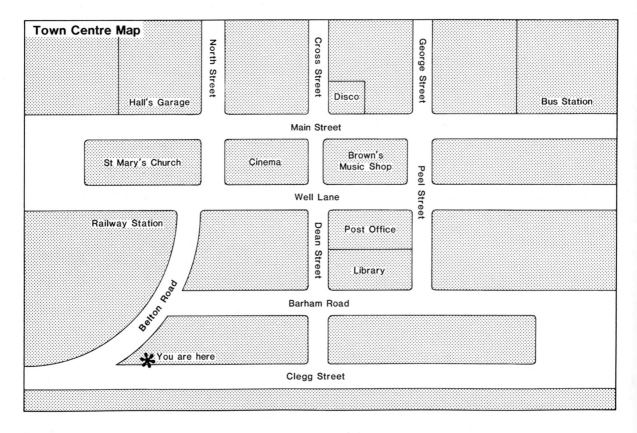

Town centre map

■ The ✱ marks where you are standing. Give the directions, putting in the street names where you can and the left and right turns for getting to:

    The Bus Station
    The Railway Station
    Brown's Music Shop
    The Cinema
    The Disco
    The Post Office
    Hall's Garage
    The Library
    St Mary's Church

■ Write out some or all of these directions.

■ If you are good at giving directions, give directions for getting from:

    The Bus Station to the Railway Station
    The Library to St Mary's Church
    The Railway Station to the Disco

Giving directions for doing things

There are two ways of doing this.
For some things you can write a list of 'do's' and 'don't's' for instance, here is a list for using a camp site.

DO

Use a camping stove.
Make sure your know how to use it safely.
Check that you have food enough for at least that day.
Check that your tent is set up properly.

DON'T

Cut down living trees.
Carve your name on trees.
Dig trenches in the ground and leave them.
Make a lot of noise, if you are sharing the site with others.

Giving instructions

■ Write a list of 'do's' and 'don't's' for one of these

    Crossing a busy road
    Cycling in traffic
    Using a record player
    Working in the kitchen
    How to keep out of trouble in school

When writing out a set of directions remember first to say what things are needed. Then say, step by step, how they are used for doing what you want to do.

■ Write a set of directions for mending a puncture. Use this set of pictures to help you.

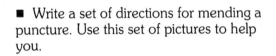

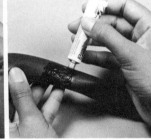

Summary

Many people can't give clear directions. Summary helps to keep your instructions clear.

Summary is not difficult. We all do it every day when we report the main facts about something, leaving out the less important details.

Here are some examples:

a 'Had a good day, Karen?'
   'Not really, <u>Mum. I've got to re-write my History essay and I've fallen out with Jill.</u>'
   'What again? What happened this time?'
b 'How did the meeting go, John?'
   'I'm not sure what you'll think of this Jean, but <u>they've voted me Chairman. It will mean I'll have to spend more time there.</u>'
   'What doing? I didn't think you wanted to be an official. Why did you change your mind?'

The words underlined are *summaries* of what happened at school and the meeting. They are the main points of interest to the questioners. In both conversations the questioner wants to know more details; but they already know the main facts; they already have a *summary* of what has happened.

Sentences to summarise

Write the main point for each of the following. The number of words you should use for each one is given in brackets.

1 John went to the garage, picked up a hammer and nails and mended the broken fence. **(5)**

2 The newsagent's was open late and Mrs Jones was given a lift into town so she managed to buy John a birthday card after all. **(9)**

3 Jane managed to catch the early train, even though her car was punctured, because she borrowed her sister's racing bike. **(7)**

4 Alan was looking over his shoulder as he ran, and he hurt himself quite badly when he hit the fence. **(5)**

5 Sally did some last-minute revision and just managed to pass the examination, but she was lucky because the questions were the ones she had hoped for. **(7)**

6 They hadn't heard the weather forecast so the Graysons didn't expect the gale. Their tent was blown into the sea because they had camped in an exposed part of the field. **(8)**

7 The mudguards were bent, the wheels were buckled and the back brake was faulty. The bike wasn't safe to ride, even though it was newly-painted and looked smart. **(6)**

8 There had been no rain for weeks. All David's crops were ruined. The potatoes were no bigger than marbles, the peas withered and the cabbages and lettuce never even started to grow. **(5)**

 **Answers** page 67

Revision and further work

■ Write directions and instructions for one of these.

a Which is the longer journey, from the centre of your town to your home or from the town centre to school? Write the directions for the longer distance. You could draw a map if you felt it would help.

b Give directions for starting a car or motor-bike.

c Describe how to apply make-up such as an eye-liner to good effect.

■ Write out the verbs in the following:

a The garage on Wellingfield Road sells petrol.
b He drove along Stanley Way and turned right into Oak Drive. (two verbs)
c Sandra galloped off down the street.

■ Adverbs tell you how or why or when something is done.

He ran **well.**
She laughed **happily.**

Write out the adverbs in the following:

a He helped himself to potatoes greedily.
b She sat up in bed and yawned drowsily.
c He looked anxiously at the darkening sky.
d She pedalled hard to get up the hill.
e Craftily Sandra crossed the road while her mother wasn't looking.
f They all went to bed late.

■ Twelve capital letters are missing from the following. Write it out correctly.

next monday we are setting out for edinburgh. we are going to stay with the jenners who are friends of the family. dad has borrowed a cortina from his firm as our fiesta is a bit small for us. we are going to stop in newcastle to see my uncle george.

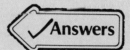 Questions on page 63

1 Go straight down Beech Grove towards the shops.
  When you reach the shops, turn left and go along Oak Drive until you come to the main road, Stanley Way.
  Turn left up Stanley Way and you will see the bus stop opposite.
2 Go straight up Yewtree Lane towards the shops.
  Turn left along Oak Drive at the shops and then left again up Stanley Way. Passing a bus stop and the 'Lion' pub on your right, you reach the roundabout. Go left at the roundabout and you come to Tenby's Garage on your left in Wellingfield Road.

 Questions on page 66

1 John mended the broken fence.
2 Mrs Jones managed to buy John a birthday card.
3 Jane managed to catch the early train.
4 Alan hurt himself quite badly.
5 Sally just managed to pass the examination.
6 The Graysons' tent was blown into the sea.
7 The bike wasn't safe to ride.
8 All David's crops were ruined.

6 Story writing

The Octopus

Two fishermen were returning home one day when they saw a dark lump of wreckage. They thought there might be some timber worth salvaging so one of them poked it with a boat-hook. The whole mass started to move and thrash the water. Two huge green eyes stared at them behind a parrot-like beak as big as a beer-barrel. The octopus tried to drag the boat under the water with its tentacles. After a struggle the men managed to cut off two of its tentacles and the octopus sank out of sight. They took one of the tentacles home.

From its measurement it was decided that the octopus must have had tentacles thirty feet long and a body ten feet wide.

This is a true story but the writer hasn't made it sound true or exciting.

Details of when and where something happened help us to picture the incident in our minds. Here are some more facts about the story.

1 The event took place off the coast of Labrador in the year 1873.
2 The tentacle the fishermen took back measured nineteen feet.
3 It was examined by a group of zoologists who decided that the fishermen had cut off the tentacle at least ten feet from the body.
4 From this they were able to give an accurate account of the octopus's overall measurements.
5 The two fishermen were an old man, James Hanson, and his twenty-year-old son, John. They had caught no fish all day before they found the octopus.

Imaginative writing

■ Answer these questions. You will need to use your imagination.

1 What were the two men talking about as they rowed home?
2 Which one first spotted what he thought was wreckage? Who poked at it with the boat-hook? Why?
3 What happened to the boat when the octopus started beating the water with its tentacles?
4 What instructions did the father give to his son?
5 What implements would the men have in their boat that they could use for cutting the octopus's tentacles?
6 Where must the tentacles have been when the men were able to cut off a length of nineteen feet from one?
7 What did the men talk about as they rowed home after beating off the octopus?
8 Where did they take the tentacle when they landed? How did they carry it?
9 How long did it take the zoologists to work out how big the octopus must have been?
10 What was done with the tentacle after it had been measured?

Re-writing the story

■ Now use the outline story, the further details and your answers to the questions to write a more interesting and exciting version of the story. Use some conversation.

■ Here is a piece from someone's version of the story. Read it through and then rewrite it putting the following in the right places.

A = adjective
V = verb
Av = adverb

1 Three question marks.
2 Seven exclamation marks.
3 The verbs fumbled, curled, twisted, crawled, flopped, thrashed, sliced, lobbed, sawed in the places marked ____V____ .
4 The adjectives sharp and slimy in the places marked ____A____ .
5 The adverbs wildly, suddenly and fiercely in the places marked ____Av____ .
6 Underline each verb that has been used instead of 'said'. You should find eight.

'What is it' screamed John.

'Lie down flat' yelled his father.

The old man and his son lay in the bottom of the boat. It rocked as the octopus ———V——— the water with its tentacles. ———Av——— a huge, ———A——— tentacle smashed across the boat.

'Roll to the other side' ordered the old man. 'It's feeling for us' gasped John as the tentacle writhed and ———V——— round the bottom of the boat.

'It can't see. Pass me the axe'

'Where is it'

'Under the net. Be quick', shouted the old man. John ———V——— for the axe under the net and ———V——— it to his father. James hacked ———Av——— at the thick, scaly flesh of the tentacle. John ———V——— over to join him and ———V——— away at the sides of the tentacle with a large fishknife. The tentacle ———V——— round and seemed to be swiping at the two men.

'Stand back' yelled James to his son. He swung the axe high above his head and the ———A——— blade crashed down on the tentacle. It ———V——— through the remaining flesh. The severed tentacle ———V——— into the bottom of the boat and lay still.

'Look out' shouted James.

He was too late. Another huge tentacle smashed into the boat. It knocked John to the floor and the boat rocked ———Av——— .

'Are you all right' yelled James.

✓**Answers** ➤ **page 72**

Comparison

The passage below shows how useful comparisons can be.

'If you kick my football again, I'll fetch my brother to you,' said Peter.

'Then I'll fetch mine. He's really big,' said Tim.

'Mine's huge,' said Peter.

'Mine's bigger than that. He's enormous,' said Tim.

'Wait till you see mine. He's gigantic.'

'Mine's more that that. He's colossal.'

'Mine's as big as a house.'

'Mine's as big as a barn, so that told you.'

'Mine's as big as a mountain, and that's bigger than anything.'

'Who wants to kick your smelly ball anyway,' said Tim and walked off.

■ Have you ever had an argument like this? Peter and Tim are each trying to think of a word for 'large' that outdoes the other. How many words can you think of for these adjectives? You could use a dictionary to help you.

fat
small
thin

✓**Answers** ➤ **page 72**

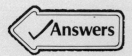 Re-writing the story
Questions on page 71

The eight verbs used instead of said are in italic.

'What is it?' *screamed* John.
'Lie down flat!' *yelled* his father.
The old man and his son lay down in the bottom of the boat. It rocked dangerously as the octopus <u>thrashed</u> the water with its tentacles. <u>Suddenly</u> a huge, <u>slimy</u> tentacle smashed across the boat.
'Roll to the other side!' *ordered* the old man.
'It's feeling for us!' *gasped* John as the tentacle writhed and <u>twisted</u> round the bottom of the boat.
'It can't see. Pass me the axe!'
'Where is it?'
'Under the net. Be quick!' *shouted* the old man.
John <u>fumbled</u> for the axe under the net and <u>lobbed</u> it to his father. James hacked <u>fiercely</u> at the thick, scaly flesh of the tentacle. John <u>crawled</u> over to join him and <u>sawed</u> away at the sides of the tentacle with a large fishknife. The tentacle <u>curled</u> round and seemed to be swiping at the two men.
'Stand back!' *yelled* James to his son. He swung the axe high above his head and the <u>sharp</u> blade crashed down on the tentacle. It <u>sliced</u> through the remaining flesh. The severed tentacle <u>flopped</u> into the bottom of the boat and lay still.
'Look out!' *shouted* James.
He was too late. Another huge tentacle smashed into the boat. It knocked John to the floor and the boat rocked <u>wildly</u>.
'Are you all right?' *yelled* James.

There were thirty-two marks for this exercise.

Did you use any of the verbs for 'said' in your conversation? Vary your use of verbs in the next exercise.

 Questions on page 71

fat   tubby, flabby, podgy, stout, porky, gross.
small   little, minute, short, tiny.
thin   skinny, slender, wiry, lean, slim.

Making comparisons

■ Make some comparisons of your own by completing the following:

1 as red as
2 as old as
3 as brown as
4 as wise as
5 as fat as
6 as clumsy as
7 as brave as
8 as long as
9 as stupid as
10 as lively as

 ✓Answers ▷ **page 76**

■ Look back at your list of comparisons, and rewrite any that you have not thought up yourself. Add more for the ones below.

as green as
as fierce as
as thin as
as tall as
as young as
as easy as
as difficult as
as strong as
as heavy as
as hairy as

Writing a description – 1

■ Now write between twenty and thirty lines on one of the following.

a A person who is always happy, whatever his troubles.
b A cruel person.
c A greedy person.

Include in your description what the person says, does, looks like and wears, but spend at least five lines on a particular incident. Include at least two comparisons showing how kind/happy/selfish/greedy the person is.

Using comparisons in your own writing

■ Describe a monster using comparisons. Think of its size, smell, skin, breath, fierceness, strength. e.g. The monster was as big as . . .
Describe a swamp the monster could be in or from. Think of its muddiness, smell, colour. e.g. The swamp smelt as strong as . . .
Describe how frightened the explorers were who discovered it and how they tried to get away. e.g. They were as stuck as . . .
Count the number of comparisons you have used.

■ Using comparisons write a few sentences to describe how you feel when:

running fast
sitting in the dentist's waiting room
you have finished a big meal
swimming in cold water
lying in the sun on a very hot day
you have not washed for some time
you have a sore throat

Pudding – comparisons

■ Read this description of a greedy person.
Write down any comparisons you find e.g. the first one is 'like chessmen'.

Pudding always carried a red 'Liverpool' bag to school. It was full of pieces of pork pie and cake. He set them out like chessmen on his desk-top at dinner time. His mouth opened like a baby bird's and in went a lump of dinner. You could see him chewing them, like clothes in a washing machine. Bits of pork pie and cake settled like dandruff on his baggy brown trousers. When the whole bagful was stowed into his stomach Pudding stood up and wiped the crumbs that had stuck on his round red face with fingers like bunches of bananas. Then off he went to buy a 25p cornet from the ice-cream van, like a duck on a pond.

Pudding emptied the raspberry juice squirter every day. It ran down the sides of his cornet and spread over his hands as if he'd cut himself.

The ice-cream man lost his temper with Pudding.

'This raspberry juice is empty,' shouted Pudding, poking his freckled white face into the van.

'Give us another,' he continued. 'I ain't got enough on.'

'Right!' said the man suddenly. He slid the glass door shut like a guillotine on Pudding's neck. Then he sprayed the whole of a full raspberry carton on his face. Pudding's legs and arms moved about like a dying bird's but he didn't get out till he looked as if his head had changed into a giant tomato.

Answers page 76

Comprehension

■ Now answer these questions about the comparisons.

1 What does 'like chessmen' tell us about the pieces of pie and cake?
2 What does 'like a baby bird's' show about the way Pudding opened his mouth?
3 What does 'like clothes in a washing machine' tell us about the way Pudding ate?
4 Why does the writer say the bits of pie and cake were 'like dandruff'?
5 What does 'like bunches of bananas' tell you about Pudding's fingers?
6 What does 'like a duck on a pond' tell you about the way Pudding went off for his ice-cream?
7 What does 'as if he'd cut himself' tell you about the juice on Pudding's hand?
8 What does 'like a guillotine' tell you about the way the ice-cream man slid the glass door shut?
9 What does 'like a dying bird's' tell you about the way Pudding's arms and legs moved?
10 Why does the writer say Pudding's head is like 'a giant tomato'?

 **✓ Answers** **page 76**

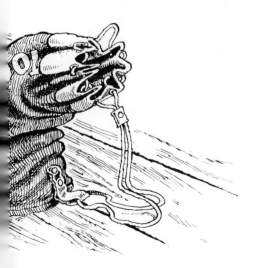

Writing a description –2

■ Now write a description of one of the following:

1 A proud person.
2 An untidy person.
3 A kind and helpful person.

Include in your description what the person wears, looks like, says and does. Include at least two comparisons.

75

Story writing

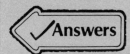 *Questions on page 73*

Here are some ideas. How good do you think they are?

1 as red as a beetroot
2 as old as my grandpa
3 as brown as gravy
4 as wise as an owl
5 as fat as a pig
6 as clumsy as a drunken elephant
7 as brave as a lion
8 as long as the River Nile
9 as stupid as Mr Cowan's dog
10 as lively as a tennis ball

 *Questions on page 74*

Here are the comparisons you should have noted down.

1 like chessmen
2 like a baby bird's
3 like clothes in a washing machine
4 like dandruff
5 like bunches of bananas
6 like a duck on a pond
7 as if he'd cut himself
8 like a guillotine
9 like a dying bird's
10 a giant tomato

 *Questions on page 75*

1 There were a lot of them.
   They were of different sizes.
2 He opened his mouth very wide.
   It was a big mouth.
   (We also have the idea that he put his head back to stuff in as much as possible.)
3 You could see into his mouth.
   It was a big mouth.
   The dinner went round and round as he chewed.
4 There was a shower of little crumbs falling. (As dandruff is unpleasant we are given the idea that Pudding's eating was unpleasant.)
5 They were big, fat fingers.
   They were bunched together.
6 He walked slowly.
   His head was stuck in the air.
7 It was red.
   It ran in little rivers.
   (Cutting yourself is unpleasant so we are given the idea that the juice on Pudding's hand is revolting.)
8 The man closed the window sharply.
   He wanted to cut Pudding's head off.
   Pudding was hurt.
9 His legs and arms are out of control.
   They flapped around wildly.
   Their flapping didn't achieve anything.
10 To show his head was completely covered in juice. His head was big and red.

Notice that a good comparison makes *more* than one point.

Revision and further work

■ In one of the words in each of the following sentences letters have been missed out. Write out the sentences putting in the word spelled correctly. Each – stands for a missing letter. The words in the first three sentences can be found in the first story in this chapter.

a The men saw some – r – – k – ge in the sea.
b The o – t – p – s tried to drag the boat under.
c The men managed to cut off two t – n – – c – es.

■ Write out these words in alphabetical order: Instant, insect, insane, inside, inquisitive, insist, intelligent, inroad, instruction, inspire, institute. Now get someone to check that you have spelled them all correctly.

■ Complete these with comparisons of your own:
as hot as
as cold as
as happy as
as dark as
as quick as

■ You have been on holiday with a cousin or a very good friend but you parted on bad terms. He or she claimed that you never returned a watch that you borrowed. At home, you find the watch in one of your shoes. Write the letter of apology, setting it out correctly. Then draw the shape of an envelope and address that properly, too. The person you are writing to is: E. Wallace, 27, Normanton Road, Wellingford, Hants. HA3 8BD.

■ Write out the following conversation, setting the speeches out correctly and putting in all the punctuation.

Mack passed all his exams Never Linda exclaimed It's the truth Sue said But he never does any work Linda protested He must have done some Sue argued Who told you Linda asked He did Sue said When Linda went on Yesterday Sue told her I don't believe it Linda laughed

■ Complete the following sentences:

a When he arrived home he . . .
b Where the house had been she saw . . .
c She was just about to get off the bus when . . .

■ Look at this list. What do you think is the biggest building? Write it down. Do the same for the rest of the list.

The biggest building
The biggest bridge
The most ugly-looking animal
The most beautiful fish
The most precious stone
The most frightening horror film
The most expensive car
The biggest aeroplane

Now use some of these in sentences of your own. For example: He looked as big as the Eiffel Tower.

7 Choosing the right word – the thesaurus

A joke

'What do you get if you cross a kangaroo with a sheep?' laughed Hanif.
   'I don't know,' laughed Sue.
   'Go on, guess,' laughed Hanif.
   'You tell me, you silly,' laughed Sue.
   'A woolly jumper,' laughed Hanif.

Can you see anything wrong with this piece of writing?
It uses the word 'laughed' five times.
Anything over-used can become boring. The writer could have used:

chuckled, chortled, grinned, smiled, giggled, guffawed, smirked, tittered.

■ You may know some of these words; others may be new to you. Discuss their meaning with your group then rewrite the joke using some of them.

■ Make a list for words meaning 'walk', e.g. hobble. Discuss your list of words with the rest of your group. Then put each one in a separate sentence to show the different meanings:

   e.g. The thief crept down the path with the stolen silver.

The thesaurus

If you can't think of an alternative word or a word of similar meaning (synonym), there is a book which does it for you. It is called the thesaurus. The most popular one is ***Roget's Thesaurus***.

Suppose it is a very hot day and your teacher asks you to write a story or a poem about it. This is what you do. Take a thesaurus. Look up the word 'hot' in the *back* in the index section. Here is a copy of the page of the index (in alphabetical order) on which the word 'hot' occurs. Find the word 'hot' meaning 'hot'. You will find a number by it.

HOR

horsy
equine 273 adj.
hortatory
inducive 612 adj.
horticulture
agriculture 370 n.
hosanna
hymn 981 n.
hose
legwear 228 n.
conduit 351 n.
extinguisher 382 n.
hosier
clothier 228 n.
hosiery
legwear 228 n.
hospitable
(*see* hospitality)
hospital
hospital 658 n.
hospitality
friendliness 880 n.
sociability 882 n.
hospitalize
doctor 658 vb.
host
multitude 104 n.
army 722 n.
social person 882 n.
the sacrament 988 n.
hostage
security 767 n.
hostel
quarters 192 n.
hostess
social person 882 n.
hostile
attacking 712 adj.
adverse 731 adj.
(*see* hostility)
hostilities
belligerency 718 n.
hostility
enmity 881 n.
disapprobation 924 n.
hot
hot 379 adj.
pungent 388 adj.
fervent 818 adj.
lecherous 951 adj.
hot air
empty talk 515 n.
hotbed
seedbed 156 n.
infection 651 n.

534

HOU

hot-blooded
violent 176 adj.
hotchpotch
medley 43 n.
dish 301 n.
hotel
inn 192 n.
hotelier
caterer 633 n.
hot-gospeller
religionist 979 n.
hothead
desperado 857 n.
hot-headed
rash 857 adj.
hot-house
garden 370 n.
heater 383 n.
hound
dog 365 n.
be malevolent 898 vb.
cad 938 n.
hound on
incite 612 vb.
hour
juncture 8 n.
period 110 n.
clock time 117 n.
hourglass
timekeeper 117 n.
narrowing 206 n.
hourly
periodic 110 adj.
house
genealogy 169 n.
place 187 vb.
abode, house 192 n.
playgoer 594 n.
houseboat
small house 192 n.
boat 275 n.
housebreaker
thief 789 n.
housebreaking
stealing 788 n.
housecoat
informal dress 228 n.
household
family 11 n.
group 74 n.
known 490 adj.
householder
resident 191 n.
housekepeer
resident 191 n.

HUB

caterer 633 n.
manager 690 n.
housekeeping
management 689 n.
houseless
displaced 188 adj.
houseman
doctor 658 n.
domestic 742 n.
house of cards
weak thing 163 n.
house party
social gathering 882 n.
housetop
roof 226 n.
house-trained
well-bred 848 adj.
house-warming
social gathering 882 n.
housewife
resident 191 n.
case 194 n.
manager 690 n.
housework
labour 682 n.
housing
housing 192 n.
housings
coverlet 226 n.
hover
impend 155 vb.
be near 200 vb.
be high 209 vb.
fly 271 vb.
howdah
seat 218 n.
howl
ululate 409 vb.
lament 836 n.
howler
mistake 495 n.
absurdity 497 n.
how the land lies
circumstance 8 n.
hoyden
youngster 132 n.
hub
focus 76 n.
centrality 225 n.
wheel 250 n.
chief thing 638 n.
hubbub
commotion 318 n.
loudness 400 n.

HUM

hubris
pride 871 n.
insolence 878 n.
huckster
bargain 791 vb.
pedlar 794 n.
huddle
confusion 61 n.
jumble 63 vb.
crowd 74 n.
conference 584 n.
hue
hue 425 n.
hue and cry
chase 619 n.
huff
resentment 891 n.
huff 891 vb.
huffy
irascible 892 adj.
hug
cohere 48 vb.
make smaller 198 vb.
be near 200 vb.
greet 884 vb.
caress 889 vb.
huge
enormous 32 adj.
huge 195 adj.
hugger-mugger
stealthy 525 adj.
hug oneself
be content 828 vb.
rejoice 835 vb.
hulk
ship 275 n.
hulks
prison 748 n.
hull
ship 275 n.
uncover 229 vb.
hullabaloo
turmoil 61 n.
loudness 400 n.
hum
sound faint 401 vb.
resound 404 vb.
ululate 409 vb.
sing 413 vb.
human
human 371 adj.
human being
person 371 n.
hum and haw
stammer 580 vb.

Did you find the number 379? That is, the section number, not the page number of the thesaurus.

It also tells you that the word is an adjective. Here is the section you will find with some words missed out.

It tells you whether they are nouns, adjectives, or verbs.

---

379 Heat

N. *heat*, caloric, incandescence, warmth, fervour, ardour, fever, n. *disease*; high temperature, white heat; boiling point, flash point, melting point; swelter, high summer, flaming June, dogdays n. *summer*; heat wave, scorcher; geyser, steam; n. *heating*.

fire, flames; bonfire, beacon fire, pyre, conflagration; wild-fire; blaze, flame; spark, n. *light*; volcano, n. *furnace*; fireworks, pyrotechnics, arson, incendiarism.

Thermometry, heat measurement, thermometer, clinical temperature, Fahrenheit temperature, centigrade temperature, thermostat, air-conditioner; therm, calorie.

Adj. *hot*, superheated, overheated; inflamed, fervent, fervid; molten, red-hot, white-hot; feverish, fevered; sweltering, on the boil, boiling, scalding; tropical, torrid; scorching etc. vb.; parched, adj. *dry*.

fiery, ardent, fervent, unquenched; ablaze, on fire, in flames; incandescent, molten, aglow, ignited, lit, alight; volcanic, erupting.

warm, tepid, lukewarm; temperate, mild, genial, balmy, fair, sunny, sunshiny; summery, tropical, equatorial, torrid, sultry; stuffy, muggy, close; overheated, unventilated; oppressive, suffocating, stifling.

Vb. *be hot*, burn, kindle, catch fire, draw; blaze, flare, flame; glow, flush; smoke, smoulder, reek, fume, vb. *emit*; boil, seethe; frizzle, vb. *cook*; get burnt, scorch, boil dry; bask, sunbathe; swelter, sweat; melt, thaw, vb. *liquefy*; thirst, parch, run a temperature; keep warm, wrap up.

Writing a story

■ Make a list of the words you know for heat. Then write a story or a descriptive passage on *one* of the following:

Lost in the desert
Lost in the jungle
Drought
On the edge of the volcano
The hot planet
Heatwave

■ Now discuss some of the words from the list you do not know or use. Write five sentences using them.

Some thesaurus exercises

■ Using the index on page 79 what sections would you look up for:

1 'hose' meaning 'extinguisher'
2 'host' meaning 'social person'
3 'hot-house' meaning 'the garden building'
4 'home' meaning 'house'
5 'household' meaning 'family'
6 'hover' meaning 'fly'
7 'hub' meaning 'wheel'
8 'hug' meaning 'greet'
9 'huge' meaning 'enormous'
10 'hum' meaning 'sing'?

■ Look up the sections for: red, rain, happy, big (large) and box, in a thesaurus.
Copy out a list of the words you know in these sections.

Choosing words

■ Now look back in your books or files on the list of words for **laugh** and **walk**. Although they are the same they all have a slightly different meaning. When writing, you should be as exact as possible. In the following exercise you are given a choice of three words. Copy out the sentences putting in the word you think is the most exact for your meaning:

■ After you have finished compare your version with your neighbour's. You will see that there could be more than one version depending on how you picture Grandma in the room.

Grandma { strode / rushed / hobbled } to her { comfortable / shabby / moth-eaten } chair.

She sat down with a { gasp. / sigh. / yawn. } Her { gnarled / veined / lumpy } hand rested on her { old / aged / decaying } stick.

Her skin looked { wrinkled / lined / etched } like an old { prune. / grape. / fig. } Her lips looked a { lavender / violet / mauve } colour.

On the shelf the { antiquated / old / ancient } clock { clunked / ticked / tocked } more of her life away.

A coal fire was { spitting / crackling / hissing } in the grate. The room was very { hot. / torrid. / close. }

Soon she was { dead to the world / asleep / dreaming of days gone by }

{ Soft / Gentle / Tender } snores came from the { big / huge / ample } chair which { masked / hid / concealed } her from much of the room.

Her cat { padded / crept / stole } in and { leaped / jumped / sprang } into her lap.

81

■ Here is another piece of writing about somebody cross-country running. Some of the words are underlined. Copy out the piece and either keep in the words underlined or replace them with words from the list that follows:

Jane was training for the marathon by doing some cross-country running. The morning was cold as she left the house. Snow was on the ground. Her breath came in clouds. She had to be careful not to slip on the ice. Soon she was going at a good pace and had left behind the town and was out in the open country. First she crossed a ploughed field. This was good for leg muscles. It pulled at the back of her calves. Her lungs felt like bags of rusty nails. She tried to relax and let her arms drop by her sides. At the end of the field was a low fence. She put one hand on it to leap it.

She landed up to her waist in a ditch full of snow, water and ice. She scrambled out and ran along a bumpy path. This jarred her legs and she had to be careful not to twist an ankle in a hole.

training   practising, rehearsing, gaining experience
cold   freezing, frosty, raw
left   departed from, ran from, strode from
was on   lay on, covered, blanketed
ground   the road, the earth, the area
clouds   pants, bursts of steam, misty patches
slip   skid, fall, come a cropper
going   jogging, running, cruising
pace   speed, trot, burst
open   houseless, windswept, fresh
ploughed   rutted, tilled, furrowed
good   splendid, superb, beneficial
pulled   tugged, ached, stretched
bags of rusty nails   vacuum-cleaners, concertinas, air pumps
drop   fall, hang, dangle
low   small, little, waist-high
leap   vault, hurdle, bestride
landed   splashed, squelched, crunched
scrambled   scuttled, bustled, scurried
jarred   jolted, banged, jerked
twist   rick, sprain, strain
hole   rut, groove, hollow

Words to avoid – 'nice'

In speech we tend to use the same words for a variety of meanings. In writing we have more time to think about being exact.

For example, we say:
    What a nice day.
We might write
    What a beautiful, sunny day.

■ Replace 'nice' in these sentences. You may use your thesaurus if you like:

That's a nice hat.
I hope I will have a nice time on holiday.
She is such a nice person.
I like a nice ice-cream.
It was such a nice book.

More words to avoid

■ Write a story for young children about a giant without using the word 'big'. Try to use as many words that mean 'big' as you can.

■ You arrive in a place where everything is very small. Write an account without using 'little'. Once again use as many alternative words as you can.

■ Write a ghost story about someone being alone in a house without using 'scared' or 'frightened'.

■ Discuss what is the latest word in your area to describe something you like very much, e.g. 'great', 'ace', 'cool'. Then describe a disco or a rock concert without using it once.

■ Describe a fairground at night without using 'red', 'blue', 'green', 'yellow'. Use alternative colour words.

■ Make a list of words you can use instead of 'bad' and 'nasty' in any sense of the words.

The Longed-for Valley

In the following extract, Mary and her younger brother Peter are the only survivors of an air crash in the middle of the Australian desert. An Aboriginal boy has helped them to survive. He is now dead and the children are facing exhaustion and starvation. N.B. kookaburra is a kingfisher; strato-cumulus is a type of cloud.

Part 1

1   Dawn brought wreaths of mist, as the heat of the sun warmed the dew-wet rocks, making them steam like tarmac after summer rain. The children woke damp and cold, hungry and thirsty, their mouths dry and their voices hoarse.

5   'Come on, Mary,' Peter's croak was as harsh as a kookaburra's. 'I don't like this place. Let's push on.'

He led off, round a shoulder of smooth-grained granite. Both children moved a deal more slowly than the day before. Every step required a conscious effort.

10   They found that the shoulder joined on to a solid massif, a great wedge-like block of hills flanked by a subsidiary ridge which ran directly across their line of advance. Atop this ridge little puffs of cloud, sun-tinted fawn and pink, were rising and falling to the breath of unseen air draughts. Mary looked at the clouds: thoughtfully,

15   hopefully. She tried to remember her geography lessons—in hot climates weren't clouds supposed to form over water? Maybe beyond the ridge they'd come at last to the longed-for valley. She said nothing to Peter—disillusion, if it came, would be cruel—but somehow her eagerness communicated itself to the little boy; he quickened his

20   stride.

Comprehension

■ Write the answers to these questions. For some you will need to search through the whole passage:

1 What words does the author use to show how the children felt when they woke up?
2 What colour words does he use in Part 1?
3 What words does the author use to suggest movement by the children?

Part 2

But the ridge proved unexpectedly steep, especially its last hundred feet. Here the rock was smooth, devoid of vegetation, swept clean by wind, scorched bare by sun. Toe-holds and foot-holds were hard to find.

25   'Careful, Pete,' Mary paused, wiped the sweat out of her eyes and pointed to the left. 'Over there, It's not so steep.'
    Slowly, painfully, they inched their way higher.

    The clouds had changed colour now, changed from pink and fawn to dazzling white. Like puffs of cotton wool in a sky of Reckitt's blue,
30   they bobbed and curtsied along the farther slope of the ridge, almost within the children's hand grasp. And below them Mary could see more cloud: strato-cumulus: layer upon layer. Her hopes rose.
    'Careful near the top, Pete. T' other side may be a cliff.'
    They reached the crest together—the longed-for crest, swept by
35   cool, moisture-laden wind – and stood, hand in hand, looking down on the valley-of-waters-under-the-earth.

Comprehension

4 What colour words does he use in Part 2?
5 What words and phrases does the writer use to describe rocks in Part 2?
6 Write down one imaginative phrase to describe the clouds and one technical term.
7 What words does the author use to suggest movement by the children?

Part 3

They couldn't see much detail in the valley itself, for it was blanketed
in cloud, but the general layout was clear. It was a rift valley,
steep-sided, about three miles wide, splitting the hills like an axe-cut.
40 Through occasional breaks in the cloud the children could see belts of
woodland and the distant gleam of water.
        Peter danced on the crest of the ridge.
        'Just like the darkie told us, Mary. Food and water. Yeemara and
arkooloola.'

45   The girl nodded.
        For a moment the clouds drifted away, revealing a broad,
slow-moving ribbon of water, reed-lined, dotted with water-birds, and
beautiful as the river that ran out of Eden. Then the layers of
strato-cumulus closed up. But the children had seen their vision: knew
50 they'd been led to the promised land. Hand in hand they scrambled
and slithered into the valley-of-waters-under-the-earth.

                                    From *Walkabout* by J.V. Marshall

Comprehension

8 What word to describe Peter's movement
does the writer use to show that he is
overjoyed that he has found food and
water?
9 What words does the writer use to suggest
movement by the children?
10 What words does the author use to
describe a river as seen from afar?
11 What words suggest that the children are at
last safe?

12 Think of other words for:

wreaths	(line 1)
dew-wet	(line 2)
hoarse	(line 4)
wedge-like	(line 11)
little	(line 12)
unseen	(line 14)
scorched	(line 23)
dazzling	(line 29)
curtsied	(line 30)
moisture-laden	(line 35)
blanketed	(line 37)
gleam	(line 41)
danced	(line 42)
revealing	(line 46)

13 Discuss as a group whether you think the
writer picked the best words for his story.

 **page 90**

Eaglehawk

Eaglehawk is like a leaf in the air
All day long going round and round in
   circles.
Sometimes dark against the sky
And sometimes with his great wings tipped
   with light
As the sunset edges the clouds. . . .
Only when night comes and the fire-beetle
   stars
Twinkle overhead.
Is the sky empty of Eaglehawk.

Eaglehawk sees all the world stretched out
   below,
The animals scurrying across the plain
Among the tufts of prickly porcupine grass,
Valleys to the east and plains to the west,
And river-courses scribbled across the
desert
Like insect tracks in sand, and mountains
Where the world sweeps up to meet him
   and falls away.
The animals live in the dust,
But Eaglehawk lives in the air.
He laughs to see them.
And when the pans *dry up and the rivers
   shrink,
He laughs still more, and laughing
Sweeps half across the world to drop and
   drink.

                    William Hart-Smith

* pan: hollow in the ground that collects
water

Comprehension

1 What words has the poet used to describe how the eaglehawk flies and sails about?
2 What word describes his colour?
3 What words describe the colour at the end of his wings?
4 What word describes the stars?
5 Why is the world 'stretched out below'?
6 What does 'scurrying' mean?
7 What words describe the grass?
8 Why does the poet use the word 'scribbled'?
9 Why does the world 'sweep up' to meet him?
10 Why does the eagle 'sweep half across the world'?

 ✓ **Answers** ▷ **page 90**

What words could the poet have used instead of:
tipped, edges, fire-beetle, twinkle, stretched, scurrying, sweeps up, shrink.

Was the poet right to use 'sweeps' twice? Would any of your words have improved the poem?

Choosing the right word – the thesaurus

Revision and further work

- Write a list of words meaning 'old'.

- Write a list of words meaning 'beautiful'.

- Write a descriptive paragraph called 'A very cold day'. Do not use 'cold' more than once. Use the picture on page 91 to give you some ideas.

- *Spelling* Complete these spellings from this section of the book:

su–prised, sent–nce, thes– –rus, sep–rate,

temper–ture, –rinkled, conc– –led, n– –ghbours,

s– –edule, exh– –stion.

Now turn over for further work.

Answers *Questions on pages 84, 86 and 87*

1 The words used are: damp, cold, hungry, thirsty, their mouths dry, their voices hoarse. **6**
2 The colour words in Part 1 are fawn (sun-tinted) and pink. **2**
3 The words suggesting movement in Part 1 are: He led off.
Every step required a conscious effort.
he quickened his stride. **3**
4 The colour words used in Part 2 are dazzling white, Reckitt's blue (this was something people used to put in washing to make it white). **2**
5 The words and phrases are: smooth, devoid of vegetation, swept by the wind, scorched by the sun. **4**
6 The imaginative phrase is 'puffs of cotton wool'. The technical term is 'strato-cumulus'. **2**
7 The words suggesting movement in Part 2 are:
They inched their way higher. **2**
They reached the crest. **1**
8 The word is 'danced'. **1**
9 The words suggesting movement in Part 3 are: Peter danced.
Hand in hand they scrambled and slithered. **2**
10 The river is described as a 'ribbon of water'. **1**
11 The phrase 'led to their promised land' suggests that the children are safe. **1**
Total marks = **27**

Answers *Questions on page 89*

1 The words the poet used are 'like a leaf'. **2**
2 The word used is 'dark'. **1**
3 The words used are 'tipped with light'. **2**
4 The word used is 'fire-beetle'. **1**
5 The poet uses the word 'stretched' to describe what vast distances the eaglehawk can see from his high position. **2**
6 'Scurrying' means hurrying with short quick steps. **2**
7 The words that describe the grass are 'prickly porcupine'. **1**
8 A river does not normally run in straight lines. From the eaglehawk's high position the river looks like scribble on paper. **3**
9 This describes what it would be like to fly in a mountainous area. Peaks would zoom up to him then drop away to the valleys. **3**
10 This line describes the enormous distances the eagle covers. **3**
Total marks = **20**

90

Choosing the right word – the thesaurus

■ Copy out this passage about a country girl in
the town. Select the best word to suit how
you imagine it:

The town felt {suffocating. / stuffy. / full of fumes.} The {reverberation / din / noise} of the traffic

was a {shock / surprise / revelation} to her {yokel / country / rural} ears.

Every driver seemed to be {blowing / tooting / screeching} his horn at once.

There was no place to cross without being {knocked down / flattened / squashed} by a {scurrying / speeding / rushing} vehicle.

Already her face felt {dirty / grimy / smutty} and her feet {throbbed. / ached. / pained her.}

She stopped to {gaze / peer / look} in a shop window.

The prices {shocked / amazed / astounded} her. They were so {costly. / expensive. / exorbitant.}

■ Add four sentences to the above passage.
See if you can suggest any alternative
words for your neighbour to pick from
(two will do).

■ Imagine you are towering above a town.
Use the picture if you like. Write a
description of what you see. Use some of
these words meaning 'small': microscopic,
tiny, wee, minute, miniature, dwarfish,
pin-heads, spots, diminutive, fairy-land,
model, little, titchy, tiddly, bit, trickle.

8 Reading and writing plays

Setting the scene

In a story, you can describe a scene in a few sentences. You can describe how people feel in a paragraph.

In a play, you don't need to spend a lot of time describing a scene or describing how someone feels, because you can see the scene and you see people's expressions.

Start a play by saying: *Scene One: A Village Street* or *Inside an Old House* or *The Changing-Room of a Football Team*.

A good choice of scene gives an exciting start to a play. Set your characters in a dangerous place or in a creepy one and things start to happen. Then the characters may have to talk about the things they see around them.

Trapped on the beach

The scene is a beach. It is evening. The tide is high up the beach and coming in.

Clinton   Can we get over those rocks?
Linda   (*Coming back along the beach*) No. And we can't wade round them. The water's too deep.
Clinton   Could we swim?
Martin   I can't swim. We're trapped.
Christine   We'll have to try to climb those cliffs.
Martin   We can't. It's too dangerous. We'd fall.
Clinton   Isn't that a pathway up?
Linda   Where?
Clinton (*pointing*)   There. See?

These characters in a rather dangerous situation have to plan how to get out of it. It seems natural for them to talk about what they see.

The opening of a play

In the following make up your own names for the characters. Choose two or three characters rather than too many.

1 Out of the shadows

You are a group of people camping. The camp site is near some woods. It is growing dark. You hear on the radio that a dangerous wild animal has escaped from a nearby safari park. (You could have someone read the radio message.) Do you decide to try for the safety of a nearby town? How far away is the town? Will you have to go through wild country to reach it? Does one of you see something in the shadows? What is it?

2 The thing in the loch

You are a family out for the day in Scotland. You stop the car by a very large loch (or lake) and get out. While you are admiring the scenery, you see something moving in the loch. Are you frightened? What does it look like? What do you do? Does it start to swim towards you on the shore?

■ Write one of these as the opening scene of a play.

The plot

You can make a story or a play interesting by making your readers or your audience wonder what is going to happen next. Create a mystery or set up a kind of question in the mind of your reader or your audience, like this:

The Stranger

The scene is a park. Taya and Pauline are walking along together.

Taya   Do you know him?
Pauline   Who?
Taya   That boy over there.
Pauline   No.
Taya   He seems to know you. He keeps looking at you.
Pauline   He's probably just standing there thinking. He only *looks* as if he's looking at me. Maybe it's you he's looking at.
Taya   He's coming over.
Russell   (*coming up to them*) Hello.
Taya   Hello.
Russell   Don't I know you?
Pauline   I don't think so.
Russell   Don't you remember? At that concert about two weeks ago in the Memorial Hall?
Pauline   The pop concert?
Russell   Yes. Don't you remember?

Even a simple incident like that can raise questions. Why does Taya not recognise Russell? Discuss this. Then, continue their conversation in play form to show what happens next.

Reading and writing plays

The way the plot of a play develops can depend on the kind of people in the play. To introduce you to the characters, a short description of each person is given at the beginning.

The Café

You will notice that reading a play is not like reading a story. The play does not give much description of where things happen. It gives a list of the people in it but does not describe them or say who they are.

George Shaw – the owner of the café
Jean Shaw – his wife
Brenda Shaw – their daughter, about nineteen
Ellen Martin – Jean's cousin
Mandy – her daughter, about nine or ten
Angie Quarry – a helper at the café

Scene 1

(*It is about nine o'clock in the morning. Jean Shaw and Angie Quarry are busy behind the counter. Ellen Martin is talking to them. Mandy is with her, kicking the side of the counter.*)

Ellen Of course, if I had this place, I'd run it differently.
Jean Oh, yes?

(*George Shaw comes in. He looks worried.*)

George I can't get the ladies' lav to work.
Jean Have you rung the plumber?
George Yes. He can't get here before tomorrow afternoon.
Jean Oh, dear! And – George?
George What?
Jean This tea urn isn't working properly, either.
George I'll have a look at it in a minute.

(*He goes out the way he came in*)

Ellen Yes. This café is a bit ordinary, isn't it? It's very ordinary, really. I'd have umbrellas and tables out at the front. Get a few flowers in pots. Make it look nice. What I always say is –
Jean Yes. Angie! When you've finished buttering the bread, can you go round the tables?
Angie All right! All right! I've only got one pair of hands, you know.
Mandy Mum! I'm bored. Can't we go out somewhere?
Ellen Yes, love. When your Dad is up. Oh – he did ask – can the waitress slip up with a bit of breakfast for him?
Angie Cor!
Jean Yes. Just a minute.

(*Brenda Shaw comes in*)

Scene 2

Brenda Rogers hasn't brought any boiled ham, yet, Mum. And we're running short of milk.

Jean Oh, Lord! Go and ask your Dad if he can run down to Rogers' and get some milk as well.

Ellen Yes. He could run me and Mandy on into town. He wouldn't mind waiting for us there, would he?

Jean I don't think he'd have time to go into town.

Mandy Oh Mum. I don't want to stay here. It's boring.

Jean Why don't you go out at the back, Mandy, and have a look at Jim's rabbits?

Mandy I hate rabbits.

Ellen You're a funny little darling, aren't you? Never mind. I'll make your Uncle George take us into town.

Mandy I don't want to go in that van. It smells.

Ellen (*laughs*) Yes, it does, doesn't it? Still – we'll just have to put up with that. Brenda! Slip up and see what your Uncle Wilf wants for his breakfast. Come on, Mandy love. Let's find George.

(*She and Mandy go out*)

Brenda I'm fed up with this, Mum. Why can't he come down here for his breakfast? I've no time to wait on him. None of us has.

Angie Quite right, Bren'. I'm sick of 'em, too. Ordering me about like Lord and Lady Muck.

Jean She's the only cousin I've got, Angie. They are visitors, you know – guests.

Angie Guests? I'd call them slave-drivers. Bossing me about. Treating me like dirt. If I've much more to put up with, I'm leaving.

Comprehension

1 What relation is Brenda to Jean and George?
2 What relation is Ellen to Jean?
3 Is the cafe running smoothly or not? Why do you think so?
4 Are Ellen's suggestions helpful or not? What makes you think so?
5 Angie says, 'All right! All right! I've only got one pair of hands, you know.' What sort of a mood is she in?
6 Why do you think she is in that mood?
7 Do you think Ellen thinks a lot about other people's feelings or not? What does she say that makes you think as you do?
8 How do you know that Angie and Brenda are quite friendly? What does Angie call Brenda? What would she call her, if she were very respectful towards her?
9 What do you think of Jean? Is she a pleasant person who thinks of others? Or is she a bit too soft-hearted? Why do you think so?
10 What is Ellen's husband's first name?
11 Is George good at organising things? Is he good at his work as a café owner? Give some evidence to show why you think as you do.
12 Give your opinion of Mandy. Do you like her? Do you approve of the way her mother treats her?

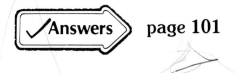

✓ **Answers** **page 101**

Listening to people talking

A good play-writer listens to the way people talk. Without any swearing, write out the way these characters are more likely to have said the following:

Bricklayer   Oh dear, I have dropped a brick on my poor foot.

Lord   (to butler) 'Ello, mate, fetch me a drop of booze will you?

Woman   (on discovering an elephant in her house) O look, there's an elephant!

Sergeant   If you feel like it, chaps, will you advance on that enemy position.

Queen   Me tootsies are killing me. I must kick off me shoes and soak me plates of meat in a bit of the wet stuff.

Headmaster   I think it was very naughty of you, William, to blow up the physics lab.

Mother   Belinda, dear, don't set fire to the curtains, please.

Art teacher   Put a bit of red 'ere and slop some blue on the copper's coat.

Dentist   Open your gob and let's have a look at them choppers.

Market trader   These oranges are not the best or the cheapest on the market but please buy some.

Write several of your own like these and ask a friend to correct them.

Write a scene – make the characters 'come alive'

■ Making characters 'come alive' in a play or a story is one of the most difficult things to do. But, if you can make people see your characters as sensible or selfish, humble or dominating, gloomy or happy people, this adds interest to a play. Choose one of the following to write a scene about.

1 The job

Two or three people are decorating a room. One of them is calm and efficient, one of them is very unsure and has never done the job before. The third person is over-confident and a bit loud-mouthed. Do they manage to get along without anyone's temper being lost? Or do they quarrel and does the job not get done at all?

2 Saying goodbye

The girl is a changeable kind of person but kind-hearted. Her boy-friend loses his temper very quickly and is a bit jealous. She wants to finish with him because she wants to go out with another boy. Write the scene in which she tells him this, trying to avoid a row.

3 The visitor

A patient in hospital has nearly recovered and it will soon be time for him or her to be sent home. The patient is visited by a person who is always looking on the black side. Does the patient take everything the gloomy visitor says good-humouredly or does the conversation have a bad effect? Write the scene.

Write a play from a picture

Look at the picture and think about the people in it. They are stuck in a lift.
Think about the people and then write their conversation in the form of a play as they plan to get out of the lift. Do they succeed in the end, and how?

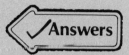

Answers *Questions on page 98*

1 Brenda is their daughter.
2 Ellen is Jean's cousin.
3 It isn't running smoothly. One of the lavatories is out of order and the tea urn doesn't work.
4 Ellen's suggestions are not helpful. The café needs repairs to very necessary things much more than it needs tables and chairs outside.
5 Angie is in a bad mood.
6 She is flustered and angry because she has too much to do.
7 Ellen does not think a lot about other people's feelings. She knows Angie and George Shaw are very busy but she still asks them to do things for her and Mandy.
8 They use shortened Christian names when they speak to each other. Angie calls Brenda 'Bren'. If she were very respectful to her she would call her Miss Shaw.
9 Jean does try to think well of people and be kind. Perhaps she is too soft-hearted about Ellen when she defends her against Brenda and Angie.
10 Ellen's husband's first name is Wilf or Wilfred.
11 George isn't very good at organising the café. Things keep breaking down. Rogers has not delivered the ham and they are running short of milk.
12 Mandy complains about being bored. She is rude about the van. She is rather a bad-mannered girl and her mother spoils her.

Revision and further work

■ It is a cold night and two soldiers are on guard. An officer with another soldier enters. He asks them about a ghost they think they have seen.
Where are the soldiers on guard? What do they talk about before the officer appears? The cold? The ghost? Does the officer accuse them of being foolish or does he, too, think they have seen a ghost? Does the ghost appear? Does it have some message for them? Set the scene, think about the characters and the stage directions you might need and write the opening of the play.

■ Write the following in alphabetical order and then check with your dictionary to make sure you have got them right:

electronics   elector   electricity   electioneer

electric   elect   electrical

■ Write out the short form of:

I am	he had
she will	he is
I had	they are
they have	you have
we are	she had
they will	it is
they had	

■ Write out the first six lines of any one of the short play scenes in this chapter in the form of a conversation, putting in the inverted commas, the other punctuation and 'he said', 'she said' and so on where necessary.

■ Unscramble these words. Then check with a dictionary to make sure you have the spelling right. A clue is given opposite each scrambled word.

ratchacer   a person in a play or book
sinovetile   many people watch it every night
udeenica   people who watch a play

9 Advertising

Jersey brings out the smiles.

We love to come home for the hols. Lee Durrell

Lee and Gerald Durrell see a lot of the world in their travels but can't wait to come home to Jersey and their famous zoo.

Choose Jersey, and you don't have to cope with difficult currency, strange languages and threatening food. Duty is low, and no VAT makes shopping a special pleasure.

Jersey is close to France, but remains firmly British. It's a Britain with ridiculous amounts of sunshine. Sports. Gourmet food. And an air of peace. Though the nightlife is lively.

The island is fresh and green, the beaches dazzling.

This year, let Jersey bring out the smiles. Post the coupon for literature and details of our fine hotels and guesthouses to: States of Jersey Tourism, Dept 000, Weighbridge, St. Helier, Jersey CI.

Jersey-the happiest of States.

Name _____ Address _____

A holiday in Jersey?

■ Study this advertisement, then answer the questions.

Comprehension

1 What two words—one in the first sentence at the top of the page and one in the last line—suggest that Jersey is a cheerful place?
2 Are Lee and Gerald Durrell eager to get back to Jersey after their travels or not? How do you know?
3 What don't you have to cope with on Jersey?
4 What does the advertisement say the weather is like in Jersey?
5 What adjective is used to describe the nightlife there?
6 Which two words suggest that there is not much industry and traffic on the island?
7 Which adjective suggests that the beaches are bright and clean and sunny?
8 Who owns the zoo on Jersey?
9 What is the name of the person in the photograph?
10 Why is she smiling?

 **page 105**

Small ads

■ You will find advertisements like this in most newspapers.

> **Camping**
> Frame tent. Sleeps 4. Hardly used. £140. 20 Raven Street Widdenham.
> Force Ten two-man ridge tent. A-poles. Good condition £80. Ring Bonnerby 2569.
>
> **Caravans**
> ACE 12 ft 4-berth tourer. Clean condition. Toilet, lights and water-pump. Double burner stove and grill. £385. Tel: Cropstone 70347.
> Cropstone Trailer Hire Co. Caravans and trailers. 46 Dale Road Cropstone.
>
> **Cycles**
> Gents Raleigh. 3-speed. Needs slight attention. £35. Tel: Widdenham 4876.
> Ladies' Claude Butler Tourer. Reynolds 531 tubing. 10-speed. Bargain. £150. The Sycamores, Bell Lane, Cropstone. Call evenings.

1 What sort of poles does the Force Ten tent have?
2 What facts are given about the cooking arrangements in the ACE caravan?
3 What else does the Cropstone Trailer Hire Co. hire out besides trailers?
4 What is special about the tubing of the Ladies' Claude Butler Tourer?
5 What tells you that the frame tent might be nearly new?
6 Why might a family of five not go and look at the Force Ten tent?
7 What might put people off going to look at the Raleigh bicycle?
8 What word has the advertiser used to show that the Claude Butler Tourer is well worth looking at?

 **page 105**

Reading advertisements

Persuasive advertising

If you look at these answers again, you may notice two things about the two different sorts of advertisement. The small ads give you mainly facts and the big advertisement by using words like 'lively', 'dazzling' and 'fresh and green' make you feel that Jersey is a very pleasant place. It tries to persuade you to go there. This is a persuasive advertisement.

Descriptive advertising

Some of the people writing the small ads have tried to be persuasive, too. Words like 'Bargain' or 'Hardly used' try to persuade you that the tent or the bicycle are worth looking at. But most of the advertisements simply give you facts and describe what they have to sell. These are descriptive advertisements.

Writing to persuade people

One way of persuading people to be interested in what you write is to use a special kind of language. People who write advertisements are careful to pick exciting adjectives. Here are some that were picked out from several advertisements for various products:

beautiful, luxurious, quality, handsome, useful, magnificent, superb, advanced, superlative, real, effortless, hardwearing, revolutionary, unbelievable, unique, new, modern, elegant, powerful, stylish, amazing, terrific, exciting, spectacular.

■ One way to study advertising is to write a few advertisements yourself. Write a few sentences about one or two of the following.

A holiday place
It could be a place you know and like or somewhere you might like to go. You could write some exciting sentences about the weather there, the beaches and the scenery. If you need an adjective or two, look at the list which begins this section.

Shoes
Look at the advertisement opposite. Does it make you want to buy Inter shoes? Why? Think of a different type of shoe and write an advertisement. Give the shoes a name.

Jeans
Are they hardwearing? Do they look good? They could be worn by men or women or children.

Chocolate
Is this a new brand? Can you think up a suitable name for it? What is special about its taste or the things from which it is made? Is it plain chocolate or does it have things like nuts or biscuit or caramel in it?

A drink in a can
This ought to have an attractive name, too. Does it refresh you? Does its taste remind you of far-away places? Does it sparkle?

Bicycles
Can you adjust these to fit all sizes of people? Or are you going to write about several kinds? Will these be for young and old, men and women? Are they easy and safe to ride? Will you mention their looks?

A new design of car
Are you going to concentrate on the way it looks? Or its speed? Or the way it saves petrol? Or its safety? Or all of these? Give it a name.

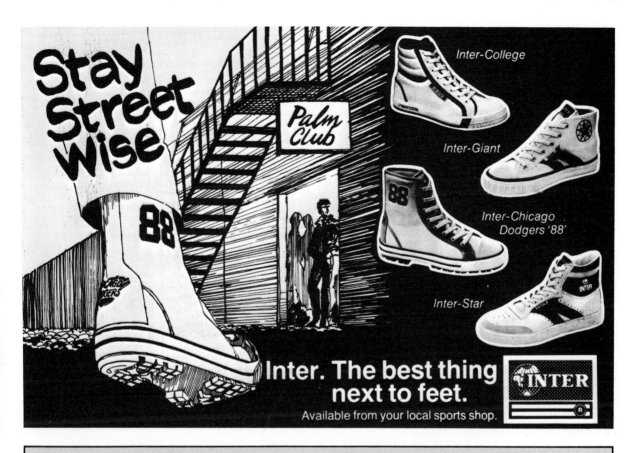

 *A holiday in Jersey?*
Questions on page 103

1 The two words which suggest this are 'smiles' and 'happiest'.
2 They are eager to get back to Jersey. It says they 'Can't wait to come home to Jersey'.
3 You don't have to cope with difficult currency, strange languages and threatening food.
4 It says there are ridiculous amounts of sunshine.
5 The adjective used is 'lively'.
6 It says that the island is 'fresh and green'.
7 The adjective which suggests this is 'dazzling'.
8 Lee and Gerald Durrell own the zoo.
9 The person in the photograph is Lee Durrell.
10 She is happy to be in Jersey.

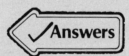 *Questions on page 103*

1 It has A-poles.
2 There is a double burner stove and a grill.
3 It hires out caravans.
4 It is Reynolds 531 tubing.
5 The advertisement says 'Hardly used'.
6 It is a two-man tent.
7 It says 'Needs slight attention'.
8 The word used is 'Bargain'.

Writing the facts

Writing small ads needs some skill in summarising. In a small ad the facts are important. But since you have to pay for every word, picking the main facts is important. Which facts? Here is a small ad, taken from a newspaper.

Garden shed 12 ft x 8 ft, treated wood, fully floored, ex. cond. £150 o.n.o. Welsh, 10 Market Steet, Marsden.

1 It starts by saying what it has to sell—a shed.
2 It might have given a brand name, if this brand name was well-known and would help to sell the article.
3 It gives a description of the article. '12 ft × 8 ft, treated wood, fully floored'. Anyone wanting a shed will want to know the size. The fact that the wood is treated means that it won't rot. The shed will last a long time. It has a floor. The person buying it won't need to spend more money on putting one in.
4 It names a price.
5 It gives a name and address to apply to. It could have given a telephone number, if there was one.

Abbreviations

An abbreviation is the short form of a word. To shorten or abbreviate a word, you use one or two letters from the word, maybe the first and last. 'ft' stands for 'feet', 'cm' or 'cms' stands for 'centimetres'. Did you guess that 'ex. cond.' stood for 'excellent condition'? How about 'o.n.o.'? Those letters are often used for 'or nearest offer'.

Writing small ads

■ Write a small ad for one or more of the following. Remember that each line may cost you about £2. If you use abbreviations, make sure that they are easy to understand.

1 You want to sell a bike. It's about ten years old, a Halford's ladies' bike with a Sturmey Archer three-speed. You clean it up but can't get all the rust off it. It could do with one or even two new tyres. (Will you mention this in your advertisement?) Someone has told you that you might get £50 for it. Will you ask for this or will you also take 'any offers'? Write the small ad.

2 Mrs Ladha, an old lady living alone, wants you to write a small ad for her. On impulse she bought a settee. It is in two halves. Put together, they measure about seven feet by three feet. The settee is covered in a hazel brown tweed with a yellow stripe in it. It looks like new and she would like about £150 for it. Make up an address or telephone number for Mrs Ladha.

3 You have some hi-fi equipment to sell. It consists of a Pioneer turntable, an Aiwa amplifier and two Taman speakers. The cover of the turntable is cracked but the cartridge is fairly new and you think the equipment is in reasonable to good condition. You want about £140 for it. Write the ad, using your address or telephone number.

Discussion

- When you have finished discuss as a group some of the small ads you have written. Consider the following points:

  1 Have any important items been missed out?
  2 Has the address or phone number been missed off?
  3 Has too much been put in?
  4 Are any of the abbreviations used too short?

Dictionary work

- Put these words into dictionary order:

advertising, adversary, adverb, adventure, adventurous, advertise, advertisement

- Now write out a definition of 'adversary'.

Library work

- Do you know what these abbreviations stand for? If you don't know, can you find out? Write out in full as many as you can.

AA   RAC   mpg   mph   hp   AD   BC

MP   GPO   JP   BBC   BR   CID   BA

BSc   TUC   UN   USA   No.   Sq.

NATO

****

Listening test two: The History of Advertising

Listen to this passage. Your teacher will read or record it from page 112. Read the questions first. Then take notes as you listen to the passage for the first time. Listen to the passage again. Then write your answers in complete sentences.

1 What destroyed Pompeii?
2 About how many years ago did that happen?
3 What did people find written on the walls of Pompeii, when they were dug out again?
4 About when did Caxton live?
5 What new invention did he set up?
6 What did the first printed advertisement mention?
7 When was tea introduced into this country?
8 How was it advertised when it was first sold?
9 What recommendation did at least one of these advertisements give it?
10 When was the first newspaper printed?
11 How much was spent on advertising in this country in 1974?
12 How much of that was spent on advertisements in newspapers and magazines?
13 How much was spent on advertising on television?
14 Which manufacturers spend most on television?
15 Give two examples, mentioned in the passage, of the kind of thing these manufacturers make.
16 Who is most of this advertising directed towards?

Sorry about the breakdown
in organisation last time.
Sorry, too, about the sprained
ankles and lack of transport.
But we are having another
sponsored walk. Let's hope
it doesn't rain again all day.
Let's hope, too, that we get
more than five this time.
Meet in the hall tomorrow.

1

HAVE FUN   KEEP FIT

SPONSORED WALK
Saturday September 18th
Morning only

Join crowds of friends and raise
money for Help the Aged.

Give your name any time this
week to <u>Mr Tomlinson</u>
Or see me, <u>Janet Edgar</u>,
between 12 o'clock and 1 o'clock
<u>today</u>, <u>Wednesday</u>, and <u>tomorrow</u>
in Room 7

2

Write and design a poster

■ Look at the two posters above. Which do you think is best? Write down your reasons.

■ Write and design your own poster for one of these things.

1 You are putting on a disco to raise money for charity. Your poster will need to give a date and a time. What is the price of each ticket?

2 Your school, or youth club or local musical society are putting on a musical. Write an eye-catching notice about it to go in a magazine.

Discussion

■ Discuss in groups the work you have done on this. Compare your work with what someone else has done on the same topic.

■ Discuss the following points:

1 Has anything important been left out?
2 Is the poster readable?
3 Is it attractively set out?
4 Are the sentences effective in persuading you?

The Longsands trip

Sometimes we need a favour. We may write a letter asking for it or we may try to talk someone into doing us a favour.

Peter I want twelve pounds, Dad.
Dad Twelve pounds! What for?
Peter To go to Longsands.
Dad We all went there last month for a day in the car. It didn't cost anything like twelve pounds. Not for the lot of us.
Peter Everybody's going. Don't be so mean!
Dad Don't be cheeky. What do you mean—everybody's going?
Mum (*Coming in*) What are you two arguing about?
Peter I've got to have twelve pounds. Dad won't give it me.
Mum What do you want twelve pounds for?
Peter It's for the school. There's a paper for you to sign.
Dad What kind of a paper? Where is it?
Peter I left it at school.
(*The conversation goes on.*)

Do you think Peter's dad will give him the money? Give reasons.

■ Write the scene again. This time make Peter work up to his request for the money. Show how he persuades his father gradually to let him go on the trip and to give him the money for it.

Revision and further work

■ Bring in some examples of advertisements cut from magazines and discuss which are 'descriptive' and which are 'persuasive'.

Look back to page 104 if you are not clear about these words.

■ Discuss which advertisements seem effective to you and which do not. Give reasons.

■ Join the following sentences by using one of these conjunctions:

although   unless   because   until

1 She couldn't go out that night. She didn't have any money.
2 The room was very cold. The central heating started to work.
3 You won't be able to use that record player. You buy a new cartridge.
4 He had to walk to school. His bike had a puncture.
5 She was a very good swimmer. She was rather small.
6 You will never learn to play the guitar well. You practise more.
7 He didn't know anything about fishing. His uncle took him out on a fishing trip last summer.
8 He never really did anything to help. He talked a lot about helping.

End of year Stepquiz

Score ten for each question you know the answer to.

If you do not know the answer you have two minutes to search through the book for it. If you find it you score five.

Your teacher will time you.

1 How many robots a year are being put in Japanese factories?

2 Name four joining words (conjunctions).

3 What was the name of the girl in 'The Horse' story?

4 What did she fall off the horse into?

5 Where was the new industrial estate?

6 Name one person for the new industrial estate and one against it.

7 Which was the most boring talk?

8 Complete this title: The Spennymoor _____.

9 What is vomiting?

10 What was the worst thing about going invisible?

11 What was the name of the hockey club?

12 How long was the octopus tentacle the fishermen took back?

13 Who was the greedy boy?

14 What do you get if you cross a kangaroo with a sheep?

15 What do you find in a thesaurus?

16 What is a kookaburra?

17 What is the name of the eagle poem?

18 What is the short form of 'they will'?

19 Where were Clinton, Linda and Martin trapped?

20 What is descriptive advertising?

Common errors

These are the most common errors found by your teachers.

CHECK THAT YOU DO NOT MAKE THEM.

1 They're is the short form of 'They are'.
   There   means 'in that place'. It is also used before verbs like 'is', 'are', 'was' and 'were'.
   Their   means 'belonging to them'.

Write out the following, putting 'They're', 'There' or 'Their' correctly in the blank spaces that have been left.

– coming now. Can you see them over –? – bringing – bikes across the bridge.– won't be any problem about transport. They can park – bikes all together over –

2 Don't put 'of' after verbs like 'would', 'should' 'could', 'might'. Follow these where necessary with 'have'. One word is missing from each of the blank spaces in the following. Write the passage out correctly.

Jack should–been at school. Then it would–been easy for him to bring the work home. He could–done it in the house tonight. I would–let him use the front room. He might–finished it by now.

3 Don't mix up 'quite' and 'quiet'. Put one of these correctly in each of the blanks below as you write out the passage.

The house is–a way from town. It is very–out there. It was–cheap when they bought it but it is–dear now. They are people who like–and on the whole they are–happy to see few people and to live their–lives.

4 Put either 'was' or 'were' correctly in the blanks in the following.

He–coming by train and we–meeting him.

They–happy to see that she–looking well.

It–a high price to have to pay and they–lucky to have the money.

What–you doing this time last week?

The dogs–running across the field and one of the girls–chasing them.

5 Put either 'here' or 'hear' correctly in the blanks in the following.

I–that he is working–now.

When will you–from him?

If you start playing records in–we won't be able to–each other speak.

–is tonight's paper.

You can't always believe what you–.

6 Months and days of the week start with a capital.
Write out the following correctly.

january and february were very cold this year.

They had one holiday in june and then another in august.

They're going to have the wedding the first saturday in april.

If he doesn't come here on thursday, I'll go round to his house on friday.

If she can't do it on tuesday, she'll certainly manage it on wednesday.

7 Punctuate the following conversation, putting in the inverted commas, the commas and full stops. You will need to put in three question marks. *Begin each new speech on a new line.*
where are you going Tim asked to the hospital Jane told him who are you going to see he said an aunty of mine she said shouldn't you take her some flowers he asked i've got her some grapes in this bag she told him

Listening tests

See page 49 for the questions to Listening test one and page 107 for the questions to Listening test two.

These two listening tests are for reading aloud by the teacher or by a member of your group. They could be recorded ready for the listening test.

One: The Spectacles

About 540 years ago a pair of spectacles was thrown on to a rubbish dump. The spectacles were found a few years ago in an archaeological excavation at Blackfriars, London but like many other interesting finds they have had to wait their turn to be restored and studied. It is only recently that their full importance has been revealed – thanks partly to the money provided by the Worshipful Company of Spectacle Makers.

The age of the spectacles is not in doubt because there is an accurate date for the huge mediaeval rubbish dump in which they were found. This was tipped behind a former river wall of the Thames shortly after it was built in about 1440.

I asked site supervisor Gustav Milne who had discovered the spectacles.

'No one knows,' he said, 'but they were obviously found by someone who *didn't* need spectacles!' I could see his point: they were so dark and fragmented (before being restored) that they might easily have been missed.

The lenses did not survive, and parts of both rims are missing, but all the important features of the frames are present. They were made from two bone plates which, judging by their size and shape, must have been cut from the leg bones of a bull.

Two: The History of Advertising

The town of Pompeii was wiped out by a volcano nearly two thousand years ago. Yet, when it was dug out from the lava, it was found that even as early as that advertisements had been written on its walls.

About five hundred years ago a man called Caxton set up the first printing press in England. He put out the first printed advertisement in this country. Naturally enough he was advertising a novelty – one of his own printed books.

Tea was introduced into this country about 1657. Shortly afterwards the shops which sold it were advertising this strange new drink on printed sheets which they distributed. One at least tried to persuade people to drink tea by saying that doctors recommended it. Within a very few years after that a man brought out a paper which carried nothing but advertisements. That was even before the first newspaper was printed. That appeared in 1702.

Nowadays the advertising industry is very big business. In 1983 Great Britain spent over a thousand million pounds on advertising. Nearly three-quarters of that was spent on advertisements in newspapers and magazines. The rest went on television advertising.

The people who spend most on advertising are the manufacturers of mass-produced goods. Food, detergents, cosmetics and household cleaners are examples of some of these. Most of this advertising is directed at the housewife. Housewives are the group which has the spending power to buy such goods.